நெஞ்சநிலம்
tamil terrains

FIRST EDITION

Text ©Individual Authors and Translators 2025
This compilation ©trace press 2025

ALL RIGHTS RESERVED

No part of this book may be reproduced or used in any form or by any means, electronic, mechanical, photocopying, recording or otherwise, or stored in a retrieval system, without the prior written consent of the publisher—or in the case of photocopying or other repographic copying—licence from the Canadian Copyright Licencing Agency (accesscopyright.ca) except in the case of brief quotations in critical articles and reviews. No part of this book may be used or reproduced in any manner for the purpose of training artificial intelligence technologies.

trace: translating [x] series
Editors, *Tamil Terrains*: Nedra Rodrigo and Geetha Sukumaran
Copyeditor: Amber Riaz
Series Editor: Nuzhat Abbas
Cover and Book Design: Prerana Das

Tamil Terrains
ISBN 978-1-7752567-8-6 [softcover]
ISBN 978-1-7752567-9-3 [e-book]

Cataloguing in Publication available from Library and Archives Canada

We ask our writers, translators, artists, and readers to question borders and unsettle various forms of local and global colonialism and coloniality. We are grateful to do our work in Tkaronto in solidarity with diverse indigenous peoples from across Turtle Island who continue to gather upon the traditional lands of many nations including the Mississaugas of the Credit, the Anishnabeg, the Chippewa, the Haudenosaunee and the Wendat. This territory was the subject of the Dish With One Spoon Wampum Belt Covenant, an agreement between the Iroquois Confederacy and Confederacy of the Ojibwe and allied nations to peaceably share and care for the resources around the Great Lakes.

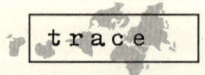
tracepress.org

Printed and bound in Canada
10 9 8 7 6 5 4 3 2 1

நெஞ்சநிலம்
tamil terrains

Edited by Nedra Rodrigo and Geetha Sukumaran

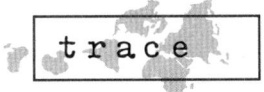

`trace: translating [x]` is a process based publication series emerging from trace's occasional series of creative workshops and community-centred collaborations. Each text in the series engages, in different ways, with the challenges of writing and literary translation exploring the ways in which decolonial, antiracist, feminist, and queer practices can help unsettle literary archives and the present.

Designed and facilitated by Nedra Rodrigo and Geetha Sukumaran, `trace: translating [x]` Tamil workshops (2022-2023) invited translators living and working with/in Tamil to explore processes of loss and unlearning encountered on their path to translation as critical creation.

Our gratitude to all the workshop participants who entered our virtual space and enlivened it with passionate thought, conversation, and creative labour. Their presence and questions have helped guide the development of the project and this collection.

Series Editor: Nuzhat Abbas

table of contents

xvii. Introduction
Nedra Rodrigo and Geetha Sukumaran

the land holds us
எம்மைச் சுமக்கும் நிலம்

02. another poverty | இன்னொரு ஏழ்மை
    shalan joudry
    Tamil translation by Geetha Sukumaran

06. the challenge | சவால்
    shalan joudry
    Tamil translation by Geetha Sukumaran

08. leaks | கசிவுகள்
    Leanne Betasamosake Simpson
    Tamil translation by Nedra Rodrigo

10. spacing | இடைவெளிகள்
    Leanne Betasamosake Simpson
    Tamil translation by Nedra Rodrigo

vazhinool
வழிநூல்

17. **Vazhinool—Retellings or Endless Conversations**
    Geetha Sukumaran

20. **குறுந்தொகை (169) | Kurunthokai (169)**
    Avvaiyar

21. • **What the Heroine Said**
    Translation by Gobiga Nada

22. • **What the Heroine Said**
    Transcreation & Reflection by Enbah Nilah

24. **ஐங்குறுநூறு (165) | Ainkurunuru (165)**
    Ammoovanar

25. • **What the Heroine Said**
    Translation by Gobiga Nada

26. • **ainkurunuru (165)**
    Translation by Subhanya Sivajothy

27. • **The Heroine's Complaint**
    Translation & Reflection by V. Iswarya

28. • **Neythal**
    Translation & Reflection by Enbah Nilah

root, branch, driftwood
வேர், கிளை, மிதக்கும் மரத்துண்டு

33. **Root, Branch, Driftwood**
    Nedra Rodrigo

38. **அடைவுகாலத்தின் பாடல்கள்**
    Songs of Confinement
    Rashmy

39. • **The Song of the Indoor Season**
    Translation by V. Iswarya

40. • **Song of the Roosting Time**
    Translation by Kalaivani Karunakaran

41. • **Song in Confinement**
    Translation by Jayashree Panicker

42. **முடிவடையும் சோகப் பாடலொன்றின் இறுதியடி**
    The Final Beat of a Lament
    Alari

43. • **Final Line of a Melancholic Poem**
    Translation by Kalaivani Karunakaran

44. • **The Final Beat of a Sad Song's End**
    Translation by Subhanya Sivajothy

45. • **Drops of Life**
    Transcreation by Gobiga Nada

46. • **The Final Beat of a Sad Song**
    Translation by Jayashree Panicker

48. **A Fine Li(n)e**
    Poem & Reflection by Enbah Nilah

52. **தர்மினி (40) | Ayalaal (40)**
    Tharmini
    Translation by Enbah Nilah

labour, bodies, and borders
உழைப்பும் உடல்களும் எல்லைகளும்

57. **Translating Labour, Bodies, and Borders**
    Geetha Sukumaran

60. **அம்பா பாடல் | Amba Fishing Song**

61. • **War**
    Transcreation by Regini David

62. • **Where is your Hand, Gnanasavunthari?**
    Transcreation & Reflection by Enbah Nilah

65. • **Where is your Hand, Gnanasoundari**
    Translation & Reflection by V. Iswarya

68. **மலேசியாவின் நாட்டார் பாடல்கள்**
    Malaysian Tamil Folk Songs (excerpts)

69. • **Excerpts of Malaysian Tamil Folk Songs**
    Translation by V. Iswarya

70. • **And Yet, We Persist**
    Translation & Reflection by Enbah Nilah

மொழிபெயர்த்தல் என்பது எதிர்த்தல்
to translate is to resist

75. **To Translate is to Resist**
    Nedra Rodrigo

78. **அச்சமில்லை | No Fear**
    Subramanya Bharati

79. • No Fear
    Translation by V. Iswarya

80. • No Fear
    Translation by Thamilini Jothilingam

81. • No Fear
    Transcreation & Reflection by Regini David

82. **பறக்கடவுள் | Pariah God**
    Sukirtharani

83. • Pariah God
    Translation by V. Iswarya

84. • Pariah God
    Translation by Kalaivani Karunakaran

85. • Pariah God
    Translation by Subhanya Sivajothy

86. **அமீரின் காதலன் | Amir's Lover**
    Kasro Ponnuthurai

88. • Amir's Lover (excerpts)
    Translation by Yalini Jothilingam

90. • **Amir's Lover (excerpts)**
   Translation & Reflection by Subhanya Sivajothy

92. சிறகு விண்ணப்பம் | **A Wing's Request**
   Akkini Sugu
   Translation by Enbah Nilah

96. **230 - Mannar | 230 - Mannar**
   Abi Jeyaratnam
   Translation by Nedra Rodrigo

98. nhilavil irukkum en eppaa
   For Appa who Lingers in Moonlight
   Abi Jeyaratnam
   Translation by Nedra Rodrigo

100. நாரைவிடு தூது | **Message Through the Stork**
   The Poet of Sathimutham
   Translation & Reflection by V. Iswarya

104. நாய்களின் அரசியல் | **Politics of the Dogs**
   Aadhavan Dheetchanya
   Translation by V. Iswarya

106. நிழல் முறிந்த மரம் | **Tree with Broken Shade**
   S. Bose
   Translation by Yalini Jothilingam

108. அன்பு எவ்வாறிருக்கும் | **What Love Looks Like**
   S. Bose
   Translation & Reflection by Yalini Jothilingam

112. வீடு திரும்புதல் | **Homecoming**
   P. Ahilan
   Translation by Kalaivani Karunakaran

116. **purananuru (45)**
   Subhanya Sivajothy

117. **kundalakesi**
Subhanya Sivajothy

118. **மழைநாள் | Rainy Day**
Cheran
Translation by Jayashree Panicker

நாம் சுமக்கும் நிலம்
the lands we hold

124. **மார்கழி வன்னி 2012 | Vanni, December 2012**
Nillanthan
Translation by Thamilini Jothilingam

126. **வன்னிக்காடு வைகாசி 2013 | Vanni, May 2013**
Nillanthan
Translation by Thamilini Jothilingam

129. **Fraser Valley, Spring 2023**
Thamilini Jothilingam

141. **acknowledgements**

143. **contributors**

153. **credits**

Introduction

Nedra Rodrigo and Geetha Sukumaran

∼

*What could my mother be
to yours? What kin is my father
to yours anyway?...*

The epigraph to this book comes from A.K. Ramanujan's translation of one of the most daring classical poems of Sangam literature and it encapsulates the work we try to do in translating. We speak to each other across languages, strangers at first, but through the art of translation, our languages and sensibilities become interconnected and our imaginations mingle beyond parting. *Tamil Terrains* is an invitation to think through land and language from a decolonial lens, one that does not romanticize or fetishize the past but looks to poetry as an indigenous practice that ties us to our homelands and helps us navigate our accountabilities, here, as settlers on Turtle Island.

Tamil is a language with a two-thousand-year-old history of poems and songs enmeshed within its indigenous terrains. The classical texts, known as the Sangam poems, form a lyrical tradition that links language irrevocably with landforms and bodies of water through the genres of thinai. This ancient Tamil poetry immerses the listener or reader in the domestic and social worlds of the inhabitants of the five landscapes: mountain, forest, field, coast, and desert. While many of these tropes may not be obvious in contemporary Tamil poetry, their residue seeps into our sensibilities through folk songs and contemporary film songs such that we carry it with us even into diaspora. However, our journey into diaspora is not an untroubled one, haunted as it is by the shadows of indentureship, war, and displacement—forced migration in the colonial and settler contexts.

This book has emerged from "Root, Branch, Driftwood," the Tamil literary translation workshops that we designed and facilitated for the *trace: translating [x]* series. In designing these workshops, we asked whether classical Tamil concepts like thinai could remain relevant to diasporic Tamil people. Our workshops became a study in the form that relevance took. The participants showed us that regardless of where we are situated, this is how we hold our ancestral homelands within ourselves—in the ecological vocabulary of our heritage—and within a context richer than what nostalgia alone can afford.

Conducted over six weeks in the Autumn of 2022 and the Spring of 2023, our weekly online sessions brought together Tamil poets and translators from India, Malaysia, Singapore, Ilankai, and Canada to discuss ancient and modern Tamil poetry and what it means to translate in anti-racist, feminist, and decolonial ways. We chose to centre our work on thinking through land as terrain, rather than merely territory, and allowed our readings of the source poems to be permeable to the effects of migration, labour, gender, sexuality, and resistance on Tamil literary cultures from the Sangam period to the present. Together, we explored texts that brought the ancient and modern into conversation. We encouraged the participants to play with language by accessing the poems in written Tamil or voice recordings for a direct translation, by attempting a refined translation through a bridge translation, or by literary experimentation that led to transcreations—poems that referenced or archived snippets of the source poems. This method served us well, as we had begun these workshops with the intention of bringing together a group of people interested in Tamil poetry, regardless of their fluency. Our strategy meant rejecting colonial models that normalized translating for a Eurocentric reader, or patriarchal modes that elevated language fluency and gender norms as indicators of cultural purity. Despite our different locations and time zones, we met online and built a community of women and nonbinary people invested in the language and its frames of reference while carrying the weight of differing histories ourselves.

Since we both live and work in Tkaronto, the workshop discussions began with and returned to the question of how Tamil diaspora translators and artists, who occupy Indigenous lands as refugee and immigrant settlers, might critically engage with, and contest, ongoing erasures carried out on the Indigenous Peoples of Turtle Island. Besides reciting land acknowledgements by habit, or even educating ourselves about settler colonial violence, how can our solidarity take a tangible literary form that situates these concerns within a transnational frame? Our conversations moved us to imagine literary and poetic translation as ongoing practices of unsettlement and solidarity, and a revisioning of translation as a practice that acknowledges the land. This work, however, could not be done without an understanding of how translation has been weaponized to erase or diminish the lives and cultures of Turtle Island. We begin *Tamil Terrains* with translations into Tamil of two Indigenous poets of the lands that hold us now. Mi'kmaw poet shalan joudry, whose poems we share here, speaks of settler colonial violence through the appropriation of land, and the challenge the Mi'kmaw take on in reclaiming their ancestral L'nu language. Michi Saagiig and Nishnaabeg poet Leanne Betasamosake Simpson speaks to the sacred in a descendant who must resist the violence of settler language, and to the nuances of sacred nature embedded in the Anishinaabemowin language. Our translations of these poems are an effort to mingle, in the Tamil imaginary, the connections between language and the sacred terrain in Indigenous poetry that resonate deeply for us as they archive resistance to settler modes of erasure.

Our poetic explorations in the body of the book juxtapose the literary tradition of love poems with the orality of labour songs in ancestral and indentured contexts, interweaving the lived experiences of Tamils both in and away from their traditional homelands. In selecting texts to translate for our workshops, we wanted to place the ancient beside the contemporary to examine how these poems overlap and speak to the relationship, or lack thereof, to the land and the idea of Tamilness. We placed classical Sangam poets like Avvaiyar and Ammoovanar alongside the early modernist poet Bharati to consider how a Tamil sensibility can be formed with land, and with a people. In reading contemporary poets like Ahilan, Nillanthan, and Alari alongside each other, we examined the ways in which trauma to land and people is expressed during manufactured disasters like war, or natural disasters like the tsunami. The rhythm and music of folk songs from fishermen and plantation workers, echoing the demands of labour and the trials of indentureship, allowed us to unearth both community references and the coded anger of dispossession. Rashmy and Tharmini's poems of displacement and dispossession described the experience of being exiled by war, one as an undocumented person seeking refuge, and the other finding refuge and home in memory, while Sukirtharani and Kasro's poems embodied Dalit and queer resistance to patriarchal gender and caste-based norms of purity. Read and translated together, over time, these poems offered us a wide continuum of Tamil life experiences connected to land, as envisioned by Tamil people.

Our translators, in turn, shared with us their unique and multi-faceted experiences with land and language. Iswarya and Kalaivani offered us glimpses of translation practices in Tamil Nadu—both its conventions and its sensibilities. Translating the Amba fishing song, Iswarya writes, "Aiyo machaan, let go my hand, / where's your hand, Gnanasoundari? / Aachi, if she saw, would beat me up, / where's your hand, Gnanasoundari?" thereby evoking familial taboos and matriarchal power. Kalaivani draws on memories of scorching sun to translate, "You say, / if the heat is back-breaking, / it is a pariah sun. / If a crow, flies away, / pecking the worm-infested grains, / it is a pariah-crow..." and makes us feel the burning injustice of casteism. Drawing from their childhood in the north of Ilankai/ Tamil Eelam, Thamilini and Yalini archive and reconstruct memories in the process of translation. Touching on the erasures of displacement due to war, Thamilini translates: "The Vanni refugee / waits for a call / from a time / when unsown fields / grow taro roots / instead of landmines," while Yalini finds a great tenderness and relief in the landscape of home through poetry: "I remember / The Saamiyadi resting after his trance / swatches of vermilion scattered / all over the entrance. / Withered betel leaf, with shrunken veins. / Everyone standing in the dark smoke / yearning for something / enchanted by the words of the Saamiyadi."

Jayashree weaves her knowledge of Tamil and Malayalam through branches of her family in Singapore to illuminate the everyday. Taking on the theme of rain in multiple landscapes to limn the familiar, she produces work that calls to the depths of a shared humanity: "You were beside me. / Dampness filled the hut / In the darkness of the rain, / a lightning band streaks the sky, / then vanishes // 'Lightning,' you exclaimed, / I looked at the sky / it disappeared in a moment / we waited for the next one, / Then the thunder roared." In Enbah Nilah's quiver, Tamil words and phrases are arrows that take aim at both historical and present-day injustices. Her words tear through a colonial trail of

Another Poverty
shalan joudry

---

i have been accomplice to your poverty
i settled land that was your territory
helped push you out
and thought nothing of it on your behalf
when you come creeping back i call you intruder
and give you signs i am not friendly
to your kind

where you no longer hunt is my doorstep
where you no longer sleep is my children's playhouse
we pick your berries for dessert
dam your rivers
catch your fish for fun and throw them back wounded
my neighbour has left you poisoned traps
while you wonder why your children die
i have said nothing

so that there be no confusion
let me say this now
you are less than us
less person
less sophisticated
less spiritual

in my defence i will tell you
i have been taught this machine
and work it automatic each day
i will tell you of the generations
of the people who were wronged this way

இன்னொரு ஏழ்மை
ஷாலன் ஜோட்றி
மொழிபெயர்ப்பு: கீதா சுகுமாரன்

உனது ஏழ்மைக்கு நான் உடந்தையாக இருந்திருக்கிறேன்
உனது நிலமாக இருந்த மண்ணில் குடியேறியிருக்கிறேன்
உன்னை வெளியேற்ற உதவினேன்
உனது சார்பாக அதைப் பற்றி நான் அக்கறை கொண்டதில்லை
நீ களவாக மீண்டும் வரும்போது அத்து மீறுவதாகக் கூவி
உனது இனத்துடன் எனக்கு நேசமில்லை என்று உணர்த்துகிறேன்

நீ இப்போது வேட்டையாடாத இடம் எனது வாசல்படி
நீ இப்போது உறங்காத இடம் என் குழந்தைகளின் களிப்பிடம்.
உனது பெறிக்களை எங்கள் இனிப்புக்காகப்
பிடுங்கிக் கொள்கிறோம்
ஆறுகளில் அணைகள் கட்டுகிறோம்
கேளிக்கையாக மீன்களைப் பிடித்து காயத்துடன் நீரில்
எறிகிறோம்
எனது அயலவர் உனக்கு நச்சு வலைகளை வைக்கிறார்
உன் குழந்தைகள் ஏன் திடீரென இறக்கின்றனர் என
நீ கலங்குகையில் நான் மௌனமாயிருக்கிறேன்

எதற்கு வீண் குழப்பமென்று
இப்போது இதைக் கூறுகிறேன்:
நீ எங்களை விடக் குறைந்தவர்
குறைவான மனிதர்
குறைவான பண்பாடுடையவர்
குறைவான ஆன்மீகவாதி

என்னை நியாயப்படுத்த இதைக் கூறுகிறேன்
இந்த இயந்திரம் உருவாக்கப்பட்டு
தினமும் தானியங்கி இயந்திரமாக செயல்படுத்த
கற்பிக்கப்பட்டுள்ளேன்
பல தலைமுறைகளாக அநீதிக்கு உட்படுத்தப்பட்டு
இப்போது வெட்கத்தை மறந்துவிட்டோம்.

and now i
have forgotten shame

even though we are all children
born into creation
given birth

in my prayers this morning
i cried your name
sent a message east for change
"for the four-legged, winged and finned"
but i am too late
too selfish perhaps
to change

நாங்கள் அனைவரும் குழந்தைகளாகப் பிறந்து
மூச்சிழைக்கப்பட்டும் கூட

எனது காலை வழிபாட்டில்
உன் பெயரை அழைத்தேன்
"நான்கு கால்களுடையன, சிறகுடையன, செதிலுடையன"
இவற்றின்
மாற்றத்துக்கான செய்தியை கிழக்கில் அனுப்பினேன்
ஒருவேளை மாற்றம் காண நான் காலம் கடந்துவிட்டேனோ
சுயநலம் மிகுந்துள்ளேனோ

The Challenge
shalan joudry

---

it's all so fragile and i'm trying to believe
an indigenous worldview
custom and relations
will survive the distance
between my grandmother and me

but it's late tonight
i won't make the sunrise
and tomorrow i will struggle to learn
one more word L'nueiei
teach my tongue to soften at the back of my throat
and make scaffolding out of language
to hold up a nation once beaten into submission
and to go on

to believe we can remember
to believe that we will govern ourselves
be caretakers of Mi'kma'ki once again
to believe i can teach my children
and that they will believe

---

* L'nueiei : in the Mi'kmaw language

சவால்
ஷாலன் ஜோட்றி
மொழிபெயர்ப்பு: கீதா சுகுமாரன்

எளிதில் முறியக்கூடியது எனினும் நம்ப முயல்கிறேன்
ஆதிகுடி வாழ்வியல் முறையும்
பண்பாடும் உறவு முறைகளும்
எனக்கும் என் பாட்டிக்கும்
இடையேயான தூரத்திலும் வாழுமென

ஆனால் இன்றிரவு நேரமாகிவிட்டது
விடியலைக் காண மாட்டேன்
நாளை நான் லெனூயி மொழியின்
இன்னொரு சொல்லைக் கற்க போராடுவேன்
தொண்டையின் பின்புறம் மென்மையாகிப் புரள
என் நாவிற்கு கற்பித்து
மொழியைக் கொண்டு சாரம் கட்டுவேன்
முன்பு அடிமைப்பட்ட ஒரு நாட்டை தூக்கி நிறுத்தவும்
தொடர்ந்து செல்லவும்.

நினைவு கொள்வோம் என நம்பவும்
நம்மை நாம் ஆள்வோம் என நம்பவும்
மீண்டும் மிக்மாகியின்* பொறுப்பாளராவோம் என நம்பவும்
என் குழந்தைகளுக்கு கற்றுத்தர இயலும் என நம்பவும்
அவர்கள் நம்புவர் என நம்பவும்.

---

* மிக்மா எனும் பழங்குடி மொழியின் சொல்

leaks
Leanne Betasamosake Simpson

---

dirt road
open windows
    beautiful one, too perfect for this world
the immediacy of mosquitoes
humidity choking breath
    my beautiful singing bird
five year old ogichidaakwe
crying silent, petrified tears in the back seat
until the dam finally bursts
    you are the breath over ice on the lake, you are the one
    the grandmothers sing to through the rapids, you are the
    saved seeds of allies, you are the space between embraces
she's always going to remember this
    you are rebellion, resistance, re-imagination
her body will remember
    you are dug up roads, 27-day standoffs, the foil of industry
    prospectors
she can't speak about it for a year, which is 1/6 of her life
    for every one of your questions there is a story hidden in
    the skin of the forest, use them as flint, fodder, love songs,
    medicine, you are from a place of unflinching power, the
    holder of our stories, the one who speaks up
the chance for spoken up words drowned in ambush
    you are not a vessel for white settler shame,
even if I am the housing that failed you.

---

* nishnaabemowin: ogichidaakwe is holy woman

கசிவுகள்
லீயான் பீதாசமோசெ சிம்சன்
மொழிபெயர்ப்பு: நீத்ரா ரொட்ரிகோ

மண் சாலை
திறந்த ஜன்னல்கள்
 அழகியவளே, உன் பூரணத்துவத்தை இவ்வுலகம் தாங்காது
 நெருக்கமாகச் சூழும் நுளம்புகள், சுவாசத்தை அடைக்கும் ஈரப்பதம்
 என் அழகான பாடும் பறவையே
ஐந்து வயது ஓகிசிடாக்வெ
ஓசையின்றி அழுதாய், பின்னிருக்கையில் உறைந்த கண்ணீருடன்
அணை உடையும் வரை
 ஏரியின் பனிமீது மிதக்கும் மூச்சு நீயே
 விரையும் ஓடைகளுக்கு அப்பால் பாட்டிகள் பாடுவது உனக்கே
 தோழர்களால் சேமிக்கப்பட்ட விதைகளும் நீயே,
 அரவணைப்புக்கு இடையிலான வெளியும் நீயே
இதை அவள் எப்போதும் நினைவில் வைத்திருப்பாள்
 கிளர்ச்சியும் புரட்சியும் மறு கற்பனையும் நீயே
அவளது உடல் இதை மறவாது
 தோண்டப்பட்ட சாலைகள், 27-நாள் முற்றுகைகள்,
 கனிவளம் நாடுபவரை தடுப்பவள் அனைத்தும் நீயே
ஒரு வருடத்துக்கு அதைப்பற்றிப் பேசமுடியாமலிருந்தாள்,
அது அவள் வாழ்க்கையின் 1/6 பங்கு
 உனது ஒவ்வொரு கேள்விக்கும் காட்டின் தோலில் ஓர் கதை
 மறைந்திருக்கிறது. அவற்றை எரிகல்லாக, தீவனமாக,
 காதல் பாட்டாக, மருந்தாகப் பயன்படுத்து. நீ அசைக்க
 முடியாத சக்திவாய்ந்த இடத்திலிருந்து வந்தவள், எம்
 கதைகளைச் சொல்லுபவள், தைரியமாக பேசுபவள்
பதுங்கிநின்று தாக்குபவரால் உரத்துப் பேசும் வாய்ப்பு
மூழ்கடிக்கப்பட்டது
 வெள்ளை குடியேற்றத்தாரின் இழிவுகளை சுமக்கும்
 பாத்திரமல்ல நீ
உன் அடைக்கலமாக இருக்கவேண்டிய நான் உன்னை தவறி
விட்டாலும்

---

* ஓகிசிடாக்வெ: புனிதப் பெண் (நிஷ்ணாபெமோவின் மொழியில்)

spacing
Leanne Betasamosake Simpson

---

the distance between
ziigwan and mnokimaa
is the difference between
singing and not singing

broad leaves are born
we relearn fragile green
waves of wind
light harvested into food
sun making breath
river washing land
lake suffocating ice
trees bleeding sweet

i've only ever seen you
hitchhiking into dreams
or running from the headlights
but today
just sleeping. sitting. eating
hours of still
armfuls of nothing
and baapase, fearless forest pilot
fast navigating, surgical maneuvering
unfolding red for the future
black for the past
white for the exactly right now

இடைவெளிகள்
லீயான் பீதாசமோசெ சிம்சன்
மொழிபெயர்ப்பு: நீத்ரா ரொட்ரிகோ

சீக்வன்னுக்கும் மினோகிமாவுக்கும்
இடையிலான தூரம்
பாடுவதற்கும் பாடாமலிருப்பதற்கும்
இடையிலான வேறுபாடு

பரந்த இலைகள் பிறக்கின்றன
மென்மையான பசுமையை மீண்டும் கற்கிறோம்
காற்றின் அலைகள்
உணவாய் அறுவடை செய்யப்படும் ஒளி
மூச்சை உருவாக்கும் சூரியன்
நிலத்தை கழுவும் ஆறு
பனிக்கட்டியை திணறடிக்கும் ஏரி
இனிப்பை இரத்தமாய் கசியும் மரங்கள்

நீ கனவுகளுக்குள்
இலவசப் பயணம் கேட்கும்போதும்
முன்விளக்குகளிடமிருந்து ஓடும்போதும்
மட்டுமே உன்னை கண்டிருக்கிறேன்
ஆனால் இன்று
இங்கேயே இருக்கிறாய்
உறங்கி. உட்கார்ந்து. சாப்பிட்டு
அசையாத மணிநேரங்கள்
வெறுமை நிறைந்த கரங்கள்
பாப்பாசேய், காட்டின் அச்சமற்ற விமானி
வேகத்துடன் வழிசெலுத்தி, ரணசிகிச்சை இயக்கத்துடன்
எதிர்காலத்துக்கு சிகப்பு
கடந்த காலத்துக்கு கருப்பு
இப்போது இதே நொடிக்கு வெள்ளையென
வண்ணங்களை விரித்தாய்

and you with your fortress of nice, trying to find something real, hiding in poetics, singing in hieroglyphics, moving around my flesh in semiotics, but never reaching out

this distance is longer than all of our lives
we go, but different
bodies return
if they return at all.

---

* nishnaabemowin: ziigwan is early spring when the snow is melting; mnokimaa is later spring and begins the moment the spring peepers start to sing; baapaase is a woodpecker.

அதோடு நீ, உன் நல்ல மனிதத்தன்மையின் கோட்டையுள்,
ஏதோவொரு நிஜத்தை தேடி, கவிதையில் ஒளிந்து, *சித்திர
வடிவ எழுத்துக்களில் பாடி, குறியீடுகளில் என் சதையை
சுற்றி, ஒரு போதும் அணுகாமலிருக்கிறாய்*

இந்த தூரம், நம் அனைவரின் வாழ்வையும் விட நீண்டது
நாங்கள் செல்கிறோம், ஆனால் மீண்டும் வருவது
வேறு உடல்கள் மட்டுமே
அப்படி மீண்டாலும் கூட.

---

* சீக்வன் வசந்த காலத்தின் துவக்கத்தில் பனி உருகும் காலத்தை குறிப்பிடுகிறது; மினோகிமா வசந்த காலத்தின் பிற்பகுதியில், ஸ்பிரிங் பீப்பர்ஸ் என்று அழைக்கப்படும் சிறிய தவளைகள் நெடுங்கொலி பாட்டை எழுப்பத் தொடங்கும் காலத்தை குறிப்பிடுகிறது (நிஷ்ணாபெமோவின் மொழியில்). பாப்பாசேய்: மரங்கொத்தி (நிஷ்ணாபெமோவின் மொழியில்).

vazhinool

வழிநூல்

Vazhinool
Retellings, or Endless Conversations
Geetha Sukumaran

~

Retellings

I am sitting on the cement floor of my teacher's house in one of the many prestigious university campuses in Chennai—it is a colonial style house with high ceilings and pale-yellow walls. The vermilion on my teacher's forehead shimmers in the sunlight filtering through the window and a serene smile never leaves his lips as he talks about literature with us—often for hours. I have just completed an undergraduate degree in Statistics and am realizing that my love for the written word is greater than that for numbers. There are endless conversations over tea and snacks. Sometimes I sit alone; at other times, I join others in a group. His home is the kind one can enter at any time and be drawn into conversation. I live there for a short while.

Twenty-six year later, I can no longer remember any specific texts or phrases, or recall any specific word he uttered. But what I learned from my teacher returns, unconsciously, whenever I read poetry. What he practiced with us, without instruction, was how to read.

*

I am kneading dough to make chappatis. My teacher is repotting a pavazhamalli plant. Her house, at another university campus in Chennai, is surrounded by greenery. She speaks to me about her research into classical poetry and explains the value of texts as original sources. Under her guidance, I learn to seek out the original texts of poems and to wade through centuries of various commentaries about each singular text.

None of this learning happens inside a conventional classroom. What my teachers gift me is this tradition of sharing knowledge purely through conversation.

Vazhinool

தொகுத்தல் விரித்தல் தொகைவிரி மொழிபெயர்த்து
அதர்ப்பட யாத்தலொடு அனை மரபினவே[1]

The author of *Tholkappiyam*, the ancient Tamil grammar treatise, categorizes texts into two groups: primary and derivative. This aphorism on vazhinool grounds the derivative as a retelling of the original text. The forms of retelling within this category include translation, summary, commentary, and expansion of the original. "Vazhi" means the path, method, or usage and "nool" refers to a text. Vazhinool is thus an acknowledgement of a descant of authors of a particular time. [2]

Vazhinool, this sharing of knowledge, is the experience Nedra and I have attempted to reproduce within our workshops, and within this anthology with its playful re-creations and translations. Our own memories of teachers, lessons, and lost landscapes merged as

---

[1] Thamizhannal.*Tholkappiyam Tholkappiyam Moolamum Karuthuraiyum*. Madurai: Meenakshi Puthaka Nilayam, 2008. 1597

[2] Geetha Sukumaran, "Metamorphosis: Journeys, Translation, Writing" in *River in an Ocean: Essays on Translation*. Toronto: trace, 2023. 156–157

we gathered each week in vibrant conversation with participants around the world.

Vazhinool moves us beyond any singular text and its author(s). This ancient word takes on new meaning here as writers and their translators include the landscapes they traverse as they translate. They share these disparate entry points in their reflections on the process of writing and translation. In this way, various lifepaths and inter-texts border the translations and transcreations gathered here.

குறுந்தொகை (169) | தலைவியின் கூற்று
ஔவையார்

திணை: பாலை

வெந்திறல் கடுவளி பொங்கர்ப் போந்தென
நெற்றுவிளை உழிஞ்சில் வற்றல் ஆர்க்கும்
மலையுடை அருஞ்சுரம் என்ப நம்
முலையிடை முனிநர் சென்ற ஆறே.

What the Heroine Said

Avvaiyar
Translation by Gobiga Nada
landscape: desert

Raging winds howl to the vakai trees as their pods tremble in fear.
A land cloaked with countless peaks
yet not an ounce of soul.
It was this cold grim path that he,
the ruler of my heart, chose
over lying in my tender loving embrace.

What the Heroine Said

Avvaiyar
Transcreation & Reflection by Enbah Nilah
landscape: desert

I can be a homebody;
I am made of good bones.
Even in this harsh, barren land,
I can be the wooden stake that marks your territory.
I can be the தூண் தளங்கள் waiting patiently.
I can be the toothpick that eases your discomfort,
or the small shoehorn that eases your feet
into the shoes you're trying to fill.
Or I can simply be the wood you knock on
when you hope your far-flung hopes
and dream your implausible dreams.

Love, after all, is a desire for the singing,
not for being sung about.

I will be a homebody.
In your absence,
I will hold up this roof and four walls.
I will cup my hands around my tears,
and yearn for your hands over mine.
I will be your pillar,
so long as you stay
my answered prayer.

~

I interpreted the original poem as full of yearning for the one who left. The emotive diction, "hates" in the bridge translation provided by Nedra and Geetha, added complexity to this yearning. Where did he go? Why did he leave? Does he truly "hate" to be with her or is it a kind of passive aggression because the heroine is trying to undermine the pain she's feeling and placing the focus elsewhere? Is the departure a choice he made, or is it because of a duty he couldn't escape? Will he eventually return? The heroine says a lot about the external world yet reveals nothing about her own feelings and desires. She uses so many adjectives to describe the landscape that the landscape becomes more alive than the people in the poem, and verbs like "blows" and "rattles" are the only movement. I learned that in thinai, within Sangam poetry, the landscape of Palai carries many symbolic meanings that need not be stated, like a Rubik's Cube that can only be solved if one knows the algorithm by heart.

Palai often features wasteland—dry, hot, and stagnant—but I wanted to capture the heroine's motionless, stagnant persona in a more empowering, grounded way. Her love may be expressed as martyrdom, but she takes pride in it. He may be gone for various unknown reasons, but this isn't about him—the object of her love. This is about the one who loves, and what loving entails, so I chose the first association that came to mind when I thought of "harsh, barren land"—that of a leafless, tenacious tree that endures unforgiving weather. I characterized the heroine to be as still as that tree, as resilient, and as resourceful in turning herself into whatever her lover needs. However, I also wanted to provide an ultimatum to recover the heroine's lost agency in the last line. She is not someone who has been left behind; she is awaiting his return. She will stay put and be everything he needs her to be, so long as her love is reciprocated.

ஐங்குறுநூறு (165) | தலைவியின் கூற்று
அம்மூவனார்

திணை: நெய்தல்

பெருங்கடற் கரையாது சிறுவெண் காக்கை
அறுகழிச் சிறுமீன் ஆர மாந்தும்
துறைவன் சொல்லிய சொல்லென்
இறையேர் எல்வளை கொண்டுநின் றதுவே

What the Heroine Said

Ammoovanar
Transcreation by Gobiga Nada
landscape: coast

The seagulls feed on small salty delights brought ashore by the sea
What cruel words are uttered by my beloved
I will not weep another day
For I have thrown his gift of bangles into the sea

ainkurunuru (165)

Ammoovanar
Transcreation by Subhanya Sivajothy
landscape: coast

---

the seagulls spread open
their great ocean wings

devour small fish in salty waters

a velvet voice shimmers over this land
it moves in landslides
    my shiny bangles slip from my wrists

The Heroine's Complaint

Ammoovanar
Translation & Reflection by V. Iswarya
landscape: coast

Gluttonous white gulls live by the vast ocean
yet feast on small fish from the sordid backwaters.
The lord of such a seashore once gave me his word
now, my bright, shiny bangles slide off my wrists.

∽

This song, when it is read as part of the *siruvenkaakaipathu* verses, benefits from established poetic conventions and devices familiar to an adept Tamil reader. While the economy of Ammoovanar's verse is stunning, this verse might appear as cryptic as a Zen koan to a non-Tamil reader having no context or background knowledge of the standard thinai tropes of love associated with Neythal and Palai.

Here, I have retained the central image of the gluttonous seagull as an implicit analogy to the lecherous lover who has left the heroine heartbroken.

The last line invites the reader to imagine how the heroine feels with the concrete image of an emaciated woman.

Neythal

Ammoovanar
Transcreation & Reflection by Enbah Nilah
landscape: coast

When the sea that beckons
all things on Earth beckoned you,
you returned her call without turning back.

Now that the sea that shatters
the mountains wishes to shatter me,
am I to deny her invitation?

My poem responds to the Sangam "What the Heroine Said" poems written in the thinai modes of Palai (Avvaiyar) and Neythal (Ammoovanar). In my version, the heroine retaliates against the "lord of such land" who would leave her behind, and hurt her—perhaps with words, perhaps with his absence. She loses weight not as an unfortunate consequence of heartbreak, but rather as revenge, inflicting pain on the one who loves her by choosing to destroy herself. I imagine that he leaves because he chooses to prioritise work or duty ("the sea that beckons") over her, but here, she taunts him by claiming that she, too, is answering the same sea that he serves.

root, branch, driftwood

வேர், கிளை, மிதக்கும் மரத்துண்டு

Root, Branch, Driftwood

Nedra Rodrigo

∼

Root

My hold on Tamil has always been a shifting thing, even though it is my heritage language. Perhaps that's a part of it—the weight of heritage that accompanies the language. I was fortunate as a child to have been able to travel around Lanka and Tamil Nadu, and the experience attuned my ear to a range of regional differences. I spoke Tamil in the smaller enclaves of extended family and classroom, and within larger enclaves when we visited Veerapandiyanpatnam, our ancestral village in Tamil Nadu, or travelled to Jaffna, Nuwara Eliya, or Batticaloa. Growing up in Colombo after the anti-Tamil pogroms of 1983, a cold fear would creep over me when I spoke my mother tongue in public, and the words that should have skipped off my tongue stumbled and shrivelled in on themselves.

There is safety to be found in "passing," and who can blame a child for choosing to "pass" until it becomes second nature? I loved the language. Tamil's comedy, passion, and often overly dramatic emotional range seized me as a child, despite the mask that had become part of my everyday. During my O Levels, we were taught Tamil literature by a Catholic nun who was discomfited by the loving descriptions of Seethai's body in Kamban's *Raamaayanam*. I don't share this to shame her; she was a wonderful teacher in many other ways but had, after all, chosen a life of celibacy and renunciation. Then, she was replaced for a year by a Tamil enthusiast; a man who loved the language in all its richness. T was conscious not to dwell on the more erotic descriptions of Seethai with a class of underaged girls, but his love for the poetry brought its characters to vibrant life. Raavanan, the dark-skinned demon-king, became a heroic figure in the way he told us the tale. No longer was the *Raamaayanam* a story of Raman's glorious victory, but rather, the tragedy of magnificent Raavanan's defeat.

I would have never thought of reading Tamil literature for pleasure if T had not opened my eyes. He did not stay for long; he was far too passionate about the language to stay out of the struggle. One night, my parents called me to watch the Tamil news on TV because my teacher was being interviewed. He had become the spokesperson for an anticaste, Leftist rebel group. I knew he would not return to our school, and that loss tempered any excitement I might have felt at seeing him on the news. That night, I listened to him speak of rights and language as eloquently as he had spoken of Raavanan, but the scale of his eloquence fit this new role better. He had become Raavanan. But unlike Raavanan, T died an anonymous death, perhaps at the hands of the Sri Lankan military, or at the hands of his brothers in the struggle.

This is part of my inheritance.

Branch

In diaspora, I came under a different kind of scrutiny, and I stopped speaking the language for years. I was a Colombo Tamil living in Tkaronto, surrounded by Eelam Tamils who often pointed out that I spoke a "different" kind of Tamil. While it was sometimes easier to get by if I mimicked them, and I did, I generally resisted the urge to "pass." I was proud of my ancestral village in Tamil Nadu, named for Veerapandiyan, Pandiyan the brave, who was hanged by the British after attempting to drive them out. I loved the music of my aunties' and grandmothers' voices as they chattered, teased, and scolded each other in that village. Even today, I am happiest speaking Tamil when their music flows through my mouth.

Many years later, I finally began to speak more comfortably in Tamil again as Geetha and I pored over poetry, negotiating meaning and nuance as we translated the literature we had come to care for so deeply. While I have a lot of affection for Indian Tamil and its literature, it is Ilankai and Eelam Tamil literature that creates in me a profound sense of urgency. The memories I hold from my birthplace of Lanka are affirmed and archived in these works and I am compelled by duty, and by love, to try to make them accessible to the younger generations of displaced Tamils born in diaspora.

Driftwood

In diaspora, we speak our language with a wounded tongue. While livelihood, class, caste, and religious differences shape the Tamil language into something that varies across regions in the homelands, a unique experience of loss haunts our language in diaspora.

During our workshops, Geetha and I shared the ways in which Tamil is rooted in landscapes, from the classical period of Sangam literature onward. However, we also needed to think about what such histories could mean to diasporic youth who grow up without being surrounded by Tamil cultural referents, ancestral terrains, community customs, or access to Tamil's complex cultural heritage through mainstream books, magazines, and folk songs. What does heritage mean in diaspora where what you inherit is loss, trauma, and the experience of learning your language in the context of racism and isolation?

In Tkaronto, I work with youth whose circumstances of learning and speaking Tamil are mired in shame. They are often shamed for their lack of fluency by their family and community, and are shamed by people "back home" for not possessing the contextual knowledge they could only have gained from growing up in the homelands. While offering Tamil heritage workshops in schools, I discovered that second generation Tamil children hold on to a sense of pride and accomplishment during the early years of learning Tamil. However, later, in the face of trying to adapt and fit in during middle school and high school, their pride and joy in their language and culture becomes diminished. This is as much because of peer pressure to fit in as because of excessive pressures from their family and community to speak perfect Tamil so as to not lose the culture they fought to preserve in the homelands.

Root, Branch, Driftwood

When Geetha and I began shaping our workshops, we agreed to make them accessible to anyone who identified as Tamil, regardless of their level of fluency. While Geetha had studied Tamil literature in university and brought a wealth of historical and literary knowledge into her interpretation of classical poetry that I found quite intimidating, my own personal experiences of the war in Sri Lanka, and its effects on my community gave me unique insights into contemporary Eelam and Lankan poetry. I began to wonder if we could make the workshops vibrant and playful, even fun, and if we could make such challenging work feel less fraught. I decided to call the workshop series "Root, Branch, Driftwood," as it came out of this combination of experience and theory, out of complicated and painful histories with the language, but also out of love and hope for the young people we work with.

Rather than creating some hierarchical system of evaluating fluency, we began with the approach that we would differentiate *Root* as a direct translation from the source text; *Branch* as a translation supported by a bridge translation; and *Driftwood* as a transcreation that was inspired by the source text or that archived some aspect of the text. This allowed us to prepare some materials ahead of each session to share with the group. We found that participants had no difficulty in grasping the content, even though they grew up in diaspora, as they had absorbed many referents of terrain through some form of Tamil popular culture, especially Kollywood films. By having people of varying experiences and fluency speak to each other in the international collective we formed during the workshops, the poems we shared with participants came alive through a wide range of interpretations. The workshops evolved into a beautiful, experimental, and nurturing space where we could each enter and engage with one another without any sense of judgement or rivalry. Our claims on the language co-existed with each others' and enriched each other.

Our choice of Ramanujan's translation of "Cempulappeyanirar" as epigraph to this collection speaks to this rare and unusual coming together in love and language across many divides: Who were our mothers and fathers to each other, and who are we to each other? But in love and language we became family, mingled beyond parting, as red earth and pouring rain.

அடைவுகாலத்தின் பாடல் (04)
ரஷ்மி

ஓயாது மழைபெய்தால் வெள்ளம் பெருக்கெடுக்கும்
ஊருக்குள் மீன் ஏறும்
கிணற்றடியில் வாழை சாயும்
கிழங்கு ஊற்றடிக்கும்
நனைந்த கப்பல்கள் வாசலில் கரைதட்டும்
வாப்பா சுவாசிக்க வருந்துவார்
கோம்பைகளை எரித்துக் குளிர்காய்வார்
மழைக்கால பழங்களுக்கு இனிப்பில்லை என்பார்
மழைக்காலங்கள் இனிக்கும்

மழை என்பது போர்
மழை என்பது வாழ்வு
மழை என்பது காதலும் பிரிவும்
மழை என்பது ஊடலும் கூடலும்

இது வேறு மழை
வெறும் தண்ணீர்

The Song of the Indoor Season (04)
Rashmy
Translation by V. Iswarya

When the rain pours nonstop
the waters swell up to a flood
fish crawl up into the village
the banana tree by the well falls to the ground
potato rots at its roots
sodden boats run aground at the doorstep.
Vaappaa struggles to breathe
warms himself by the fire
burning coconut shells.
"The fruits of the monsoon
lack sweetness," he says.
Sweet is the season of rains.

Rain means war.
Rain means life.
Rain means loving and leaving.
Rain means to wrangle and to reconcile.

This rain is different:
Just water.

Song of the Roosting Time (04)

Rashmy

Translation by Kalaivani Karunakaran

When it pours, heavy
floods overflow
fish stream into the village
the plantain beside the well falls
potatoes rot
drenched ships run aground.
Vaappaa finds it difficult to breathe
burns coconut shells to keep warm.

Monsoon fruits lack sweetness
he says
but monsoons taste sweet.

Rain is war.
Rain is life.
Rain is love and separation.
Rain is the lovers' tiff and reunion.

This rain is different
It's mere water.

Song in Confinement (04)

Rashmy
Translation by Jayashree Panicker

When the rains do not stop
waters surge
fish swim into the village
the banana tree sags at the foot of the well
the potato rots
soaked boats perch at the doorway.
Vaappaa has difficulty breathing
he burns coconuts
to keep warm.
Monsoon fruits are not sweet, he says
monsoon times are sweet.

War is rain.
Life is rain.
Loving and letting go is rain.
Rain is the sulks and sweetness of lovers.

This is a different rain.
It is just water.

முடிவடையும் சோகப் பாடலொன்றின் இறுதி அடி
அலரி

நெடுநாட்களுக்குப் பின்னொரு இராக்காலம்
பேரலைகள் விழுங்கிய ஊர்க்கரையை
தனியே காணச் சென்றிருந்தேன்.

முடிவற்ற துயரின் ஓவியங்களாக
எல்லாம் காட்சி தந்தன.

உடைந்திருக்கும் வீடுகளில்
முற்றங்களில்
கரிய இருள் எழுந்து படர்ந்தது.
குப்பிவிளக்கொன்றை ஏற்றிடக் கூட சுவர்களில்லை
ஆட்களில்லை.

முறிந்திருக்கும் தென்னைகளின்
பனைகளின்
தெருக்களின்
மேலாக ஓசையற்ற காற்று தனித்தலைந்தது.

இறக்கை தொலைத்த கடற்பட்சிகள்
திசைகெட்டு
கடலை ஒடுங்கிக் கடந்தன.

முடிவடையும் சோகப் பாடலொன்றின்
இறுதி அடியாக
எல்லாமே இறந்து காட்சியளித்தன.

மங்கிக் குருடாகும் நிலவின் மஞ்சள் இருளில்
விபரிக்க முடியா வேதனை சுமந்து
வீடு திரும்பிக் கொண்டிருந்தேன்.
என்னையும் இழந்து.

Final Line of a Melancholic Poem
Alari
Translation by Kalaivani Karunakaran

On a night
after several days
I went alone
to see the wave-devoured village,
a portrait of
an ever-lasting grief.

Darkness shrouds
the broken houses, courtyards
with no one to light a glass lamp.
A lonely wind wanders through
the broken streets,
coconut trees, and palmyras,
everything looks lifeless.

I trudge back home
heavy with grief
under the diminishing, blinding
moonlight,
losing my own self.

The Final Beat of a Sad Song's End
Alari
Translation by Subhanya Sivajothy

Many days passed
alone, I visited the wrung-out villages.

Colours of blue and grey billow
into each other.

In the shattered houses a dark centre
bloomed and spread. How does one
light a lamp in a house that has no walls.

Broken palmyras forage for a root to hold on to.
A resigned wind smoothes over the sharp
edges of decay.

The disoriented seabirds, the missing people,

the last word of a sad song. The final beat.
Everything lifeless in their silence.

The blurring moon dims yellow in the darkness,
an inarticulate anguish smouldering on my back,
I return home, having lost myself too.

Drops of Life
Alari
Transcreation by Gobiga Nada

It ends and begins in the mighty ocean
Sometimes the waves gently caress the land, sometimes they shove
Such bewildering love between the land and the sea
Until the day the ocean's fury overtakes its calm, and doom arrives
It was heaven on earth...
Now, an island ravaged

Broken limbs
Broken boats
Broken homes
Broken hopes
... (pause, silence)

Drops of life
Flood of havoc
Pulse of the earth
Creator and Destroyer
Draped in shades of celestial blue
But arriving like fire
Swooping in to snatch all of life's force
Leaving nothing but drops of blood
Seeping into the ocean

Drops of blood then mingle with drops of water
Then once again turn into drops of life

The Final Beat of a Sad Song
Alari
Translation by Jayashree Panicker

One night, many nights later
I went by myself to see the shore
swallowed by huge waves.

Everything appeared to be a
painting of endless sorrow.

In the broken houses
in the front yards
darkness rose and spread.
There wasn't any wall
nor anyone
to raise a kerosene lamp.

A silent wind
wandered over the
broken coconut trees
the palmyra trees
and the streets.

The seagulls
having lost their wings
retreated from the sea
directionless.

Everything seemed dead
like the final beat
of a sad song.

In the dimming glow
of the waning moon
carrying an indescribable
sorrow within me
I returned home
having lost myself too.

A Fine Li(n)e

Poem & Reflection by Enbah Nilah

What are
borders
but
barriers   li(n)es   routes
to prevent   to punish   to police   to violate
the arrival of   the scourge of   the exodus of   the rights of   the dignity of
illegal   foreign   war-torn   devastated   desperate
people   children   families   humans
dying for   hoping for   praying for
a place   a land
that promises
home?

Can the sons of soil
point out a document more
legitimate   honest   unimpeachable
than the scars borne from
building   carrying   fleeing with
a country
on your back?

Can the patriots
point out a democracy more
equalizing   autonomous   unwavering
than that of
a virus   a famine   a flood   a drought?

Can a passport and a visa
adequately explain what it's like to
live with   move between   raise a child in
split
tongues   souls   worlds?

If life on Earth
began   evolved   will end
in the depths of the ocean,
what power do the sons of soil have
to declare us
aliens?

∼

In this poem, I experiment with graphological deviations, with the visual motif of floating icebergs to symbolise all that is submerged in discussions about the movement of refugees. Interestingly, Geetha interpreted the poem's visual structure as a human body, an interpretation I loved. I wanted the poem, particularly its first stanza, to make sense regardless of how it is read, whether horizontally, vertically, or diagonally, or by picking and choosing words to fill in its blanks.

I wrote to question the politics of linguistic ambiguity and its very real consequences on people who live on the margins. Nedra interpreted the white spaces in the text as water, given that the text begins with questions of who belongs to the soil, and ends with a return to the sea. Refugees and asylum seekers are often represented as being adrift at sea in rickety boats, hoping to reach a land that will serve as their new haven. Yet time and time again, we hear stories of migrants drowning as they attempt the treacherous journey.

The poem's spaces can also be read as silence, as space to breathe, reflect, and rest within the pervasive, relentless violence that the poem presents. In every text we read, be it on paper, a billboard, or a screen, countless words and voices flood and inform our judgement of the world. When the language we use is inherently contentious and polarising, the space between words becomes a welcome respite, a much-needed pause from such constant bombardment. We make meaning even from the nothingness on a page.

There's a lot to be said about the resilience of humans and our capacity to pull through even the worst of situations. Refugees and migrants may lose a home, a history, a language, an identification, even their people, yet still find meaning in the barrenness between losses.

அயலாள் (40)
தர்மினி

ஆமி வருகிறது ஓடு
ஷெல் விழுகிறது ஓடு
சில மணித்தியாலங்களில் ஊரை விட்டு ஓடு
படகேறி ஓடு
விமானமேறி ஓடு
கடவுச்சீட்டு கொடு
கைரேகை வை
மொழி தெரியாதா
உலக வரைபடத்தில் உன் நாடு அதோ
இந்நாடு இதோ
இவ்வளவு தூரம் ஓடிவந்த செலவென்ன?
உன் உயிராபத்துக்குக் காரணம் காட்டு
அகதியாவதற்கு ஆதாரங்கள் என்னென்ன
விண்ணப்பம் மறுக்கப்பட்டது
திரும்பிப் போ
அடையாள அட்டை எங்கே?
வீஸா இருக்கிறதா?
வேலை செய்கிறாயா?
"நல்ல தொழிலாளி"
இருந்துவிட்டுப் போ

Ayalaal (40)

Tharmini

Translation by Enbah Nilah

Run, the Army is coming.
Run, shells are falling.
Flee the village within hours.
Flee by boats.
Flee by flights.
Give me your passport.
Mark your fingerprint.
Don't you know the language?
There is your country
on the world map.
And here is our country.
What was the expense of this long travel?
Show us the reasons for your persecution.
What is the evidence
for you becoming a refugee?
Application rejected.
Go back.
Where is your ID?
Do you have a visa?
Will you work?
"A good labourer"
You are "permitted" to stay.

labour, bodies, and borders
உழைப்பும் உடல்களும் எல்லைகளும்

Translating Labour, Bodies, and Borders

Geetha Sukumaran

∼

Shoulders and hands move in unison to drag the fishing net from the sea. Legs move in patterned steps to support upper bodies and feet across wet, slippery sand. As the boat thrusts out into the sea with multiple hands holding their oars and rowing in harmony, songs splash through the sounds of water. Blue of ocean and sky, shimmering colours of sea life, golden sand, and dark male bodies—fishing is shared labour, with shared words, colours, sights, and rhythmic sounds.

It is a universal phenomenon to associate sound with bodily movement. Each culture has its own sounds associated with the rhythm of the body, depending on the labour that the work demands, and the movement of the body across landscapes. A body engaged in fishing internalizes the ebb and flow of the ocean and learns to incorporate it in its movements. Its agitation, then, expresses the way the human body and the water body interact, negotiate, and harmonize with each other. The stirring of hands, the beads of sweat, and salt on the tongue embody the ocean's movements.

Here, in this physical act, limbs, words, emotions, and lyrical conversations with quick, quirky retorts, fuse to create a domain of human rhythm and music. The roar of the waves, the exhale of the conch shell, the flapping of fish and other ocean sounds form nature's melody. They come together when the inhabitants of the two landscapes encounter each other. These terrains, humans, species, and microbes are all intimately associated with the labour of fishing.

What does it mean to translate this realm of unison? How does one express the sweat of the toiling male body and the salt of sand and sea breeze? Translation, here, is the act of interpreting the ocean as communicated by men. Traditionally, women do not go into the sea to fish but work in the marketplace as sellers of the catch. The multi-sensory world of the ocean finds meaning primarily through words at work from the still, land-bound bodies of women and nonbinary people. The bodies that translate work at a distance from the rhythmic movements of labouring male bodies, crashing waves, and the soft breathing of the sea's life. Their quiet bodies are juxtaposed with the sounds of life.

Translation happens here, in this silence, on a notebook or a laptop. The laptop screen may sometimes be filled with a screensaver of a silent sea… recreating its songs in another language in which the varied physiological senses as well as the salt, the vibrant hues, and the ocean's rhythm resonate from the soul of a faraway translator. Like the fisherwomen, the translator engages with bodily labour without ever experiencing the sea, yet takes it to the public. The songs of the coast reach inland and cross terrains through re-creations into another language. The music that arrives in the poem, rendered into English, is a translation of all these movements and landscapes flowing into one another.

குருநகரின் அம்பா பாடல், யாழ்ப்பாணம்

ஏலம்மா ஏலேதண்டு கை எங்கே ஞானசவுந்தரி

ஓவலம்மா ஏலேதண்டு கை எங்கே ஞானசவுந்தரி

வருகுதடா கப்பலொண்டு கை எங்கே ஞானசவுந்தரி

வாழக்காய் பாரமேத்தி கை எங்கே ஞானசவுந்தரி

ஐயோமச்சான் கையையிவிடு கை எங்கே ஞானசவுந்தரி

ஆச்சிகண்டா அடிக்கப்போறா கை எங்கே ஞானசவுந்தரி

எடுக்கிறேன்பார் கத்தியொண்டு கை எங்கே ஞானசவுந்தரி

குத்திறேன்பார் நெஞ்சினிலே கை எங்கே ஞானசவுந்தரி

அண்ணேவா திண்ணையிலே கை எங்கே ஞானசவுந்தரி

அரசன்வா மூலையிலே கை எங்கே ஞானசவுந்தரி

கள்ளனடா யாக்கோப்பன் கை எங்கே ஞானசவுந்தரி

கதவருகே நிக்கிறான்ரா கை எங்கே ஞானசவுந்தரி

நிலவு படுந்தனையும் கை எங்கே ஞானசவுந்தரி

நின்றாரடி வாசலிலே கை எங்கே ஞானசவுந்தரி

இழுக்கிறேன்பார் என்ரபக்க கை எங்கே ஞானசவுந்தரி

எடுக்கிறேன்பார் ரண்டுசோடா கை எங்கே ஞானசவுந்தரி

War

Amba song from Gurunagar, Jaffna
Transcreation by Regini David

*Elamma elethandu, where is your hand,
Gnanasavunthari?*

Dark nights of terror become our life

*Elamma elethandu, where is your hand,
Gnanasavunthari?*

Our blue sky turns black

*Elamma elethandu, where is your hand,
Gnanasavunthari?*

Green pastures turn red

*Elamma elethandu, where is your hand,
Gnanasavunthari?*

Our tears, a river of darkness

*Elamma elethandu, where is your hand,
Gnanasavunthari?*

I searched the ocean for fish

*Elamma elethandu, where is your hand,
Gnanasavunthari?*

I was met with a river of blood

*Elamma elethandu, where is your hand,
Gnanasavunthari?*

Where is your hand, Gnanasavunthari?

Amba song from Gurunagar, Jaffna
Transcreation & Reflection by Enbah Nilah

Eyes turned to sea, back to the land,
our old country turned her back on us.
Where is your hand, Gnanasavunthari?

No more than goats and cattle,
you let them take us, then break us.
Where is your hand, Gnanasavunthari?

I don't hear my mother(land) call,
I wonder what is the matter.
Where is your hand, Gnanasavunthari?

Are my people still well back home?
Or have they, like seeds, scattered?
Where is your hand, Gnanasavunthari?

Tapped my way through the plantations,
I have bled more than the rubber trees.
Where is your hand, Gnanasavunthari?

My arms and legs have lost feelings,
still no one reaches out for me.
Where is your hand, Gnanasavunthari?

I harvest the sugar canes, but
the white man calls me by a different name.
Where is my name, Gnanasavunthari?

I cut my hand on the sickle,
the white man threatens to cut my head.
Where is *my* hand, Gnanasavunthari?

When you call out "Amma,"
Mother Mary hands down a miracle.
There is your hand, Gnanasavunthari.

When I call out for mine,
a man's boot damn near cracks my spine.
Where is my God, Gnanasavunthari?

You've lost only hands, we're nothing but hands;
the land remembers all but us.
Where is my land, Gnanasavunthari?

I know even God gets tired,
tired of looking down at us.
You can have my hands, Gnanasavunthari.

∼

My poem is inspired by an Amba fishing song that originates from Gurunagar in Jaffna, Sri Lanka. This labour song unfolds with a series of couplets and a refrain alluding to the Christian folk tale of the princess Gnanasavunthari who is an ardent devotee of the Virgin Mary. Gnanasavunthari's stepmother concocts a plan to murder the princess but the men she hires cut off the princess's arms and leave her alive in the forest, returning with a false report of her death. Gnanasavunthari then prays to Mother Mary who descends to save her and returns her arms to her body.

This story made me reflect on continuity and fragmentation within the song itself, and on how the experience of labour can be vastly different when one feels connected to the land and the sea one labours in, and finds sustenance within.

Even though working the land is backbreaking regardless of location, those who can claim ownership to the land may find it rewarding, at least on a spiritual level. But those who are displaced and labouring elsewhere under foreign supervision, without a sense of community, are dehumanized and alienated from the fruits of their labour. I wanted to use the metaphor of the severing of limbs to convey the rootlessness of indentured labourers. I took the creative liberty of turning Gnanasavunthari into the medium between God and the Godforsaken since she, as a princess and a mythical figure, was fortunate enough to have her prayers answered.

The same cannot be said for some of our ancestors.

Where's your hand, Gnanasoundari?

Amba song from Gurunagar, Jaffna
Translation & Reflection by V. Iswarya

Elamma elethandu,
where's your hand, Gnanasoundari?
Ovalamma elethandu,
where's your hand, Gnanasoundari?
Look, here's a ship coming,
where's your hand, Gnanasoundari?
Laden with plantain in it,
where's your hand, Gnanasoundari?
Aiyo machaan, let go my hand,
where's your hand, Gnanasoundari?
Aachi, if she saw, would beat me up,
where's your hand, Gnanasoundari?
Here, look, as I draw out a knife,
where's your hand, Gnanasoundari?
Hey, I shall stick it in the chest,
where's your hand, Gnanasoundari?
You brother, come to the porch,
where's your hand, Gnanasoundari?
You king, come to the corner,
where's your hand, Gnanasoundari?
Jacob, there, is a right crook,
where's your hand, Gnanasoundari?
He stands there beside the door,
where's your hand, Gnanasoundari?
The moon sinks under the sea,
where's your hand, Gnanasoundari?
Standing there by the gate,
where's your hand, Gnanasoundari?

See, I shall pull on my side,
where's your hand, Gnanasoundari?
See, I shall pull out two sodas,
where's your hand, Gnanasoundari?

∼

Amba songs are traditional songs of labour sung by Tamil fishermen during their trips on manually operated boats. The rhythm of these songs is aligned with the movement of the body and the line lengths are determined by the collective effort needed to pull the fishing nets uniformly from the sea. Amba[1] might simply mean a beautiful song or a song in praise of the Sea Goddess.[2]

In the process of translating this song, I listened to several video recordings documenting Amba fishing songs to learn how their rhythm aligned with the labour the singers were engaged in. Despite the singers being all male, the songs usually contain a common refrain with female names such as "Rosa," "Laila," or "Gnanasoundari." Given the backdrop of their manual labour, their invocation of Gnanasoundari in the song becomes especially poignant.

The legend of Gnanasoundari is popular among Tamil-speaking Catholic communities, telling the story of the young princess Gnanasoundari who was abandoned in a forest with both her hands amputated due to the evil plans of her stepmother. An ardent devotee of Virgin Mary, the girl prayed to her to be rescued and soon had both her arms restored. So, this song becomes a form of prayer for the pious, acknowledging the bounty of the goddess, while retaining the reminder that it is the labour of their hands that ultimately feeds them.

---

[1] M. Pusparajan. *Ampa: Essays on Fishermen's Folk Songs.* Jaffna: Alai Literary Circle, 1976. 3

[2] N. Vanamamalai. ed. *Thamizhar Nattup Padalgal.* 6th ed. Chennai: New Century Book House, 2006. 446

மலேசியாவின் நாட்டார் பாடல்கள்

1
ஆட்டு மாட்டு மந்தையைப் போல
ஆங்கிலேயர்களும் நம்மை
கூட்டில் அடைத்து வைத்து
கொடுமைகள் செய்கின்றாரே

2
கரும்பு தோட்டத்திலே — நம் இந்தியரை
கூலியெனும் பெயர்கொடுத்து
கொண்டுபோறார் பதிவு செய
ரயில்ல ஏத்தி

3
கஷ்டப்பட்டோமே பத்து வெள்ளிதான்
கொடுத்து ரயில்ல ஏத்தினான்
சேலை பேனு சொறி சிரங்கு — நாங்க
நொந்து வாழ்றோம்

Excerpts of Malaysian Tamil Folk Songs
Translation by V. Iswarya

1
Herded and hemmed in
like cattle and goats are we
the British bind us in cages
they beat us to break our spirits.

2
They call us coolies—
we Indian folk in sugarcane fields.
They bundle us into trains
to register our names.

3
How we suffered for those ten dollars
they gave when they put us on a train!
Lice on our clothes, skin sore with scabies—
our lives go on, labouring in agony.

And Yet, We Persist

Translation & Reflection by Enbah Nilah

1
No different from herding
goats and cattle
the English cage us
and abuse us.

2
In the sugarcane plantations
we, the Indians
are renamed coolies
flocked into trains
then taken to be branded.

3
They paid only ten coins
the price of our agony
then rounded us up on trains.
Lice in our clothes, itching scabies—
in pain
yet we persist.

∽

This poem-song is relatively simple in language, despite the weight of the topic. I wanted to extend the metaphor of herding throughout my translation to accentuate the dehumanization of these labourers, so I picked verbs that connote animal rearing beyond the first stanza, e.g., flocked, branded, rounded up.

I took some creative liberties with the last line by choosing the word "persist" instead of "live" because the quality of life described in the poem is atrocious and can only be endured. That said, I wondered if, in doing so, I ascribe a sense of meaninglessness to these very real lived experiences of the labourers. Who am I to decide what kind of life is worth "living"?

After contemplating the last line for a long time, I decided to retain the word "persist." The moral burden and ignominy of deciding whose lives are worthy of being called such is not on me, but on the colonizers. These labourers are not lesser humans because of the way they were treated. In fact, they were more human than most, for they not only found the will to survive in hostile conditions, but also the creative impetus to immortalize their lives through oral storytelling or songs. This translation is rather an indictment of the colonizers—the perpetrators of violence who have lost their own humanity as a result of their desire to oppress another member of the human family.

மொழிபெயர்த்தல் என்பது எதிர்த்தல்
to translate is to resist

To Translate is to Resist
Nedra Rodrigo

∽

I could not enter the practice of translation feigning ignorance of the myriad ways in which translation has served as a tool of surveillance, categorization, and suppression. As much as translation has enriched our lives with glimpses into the richness of other cultures, their sensibilities, and struggles, it has also served to impoverish many of those cultures through the violences of settler colonialism and extraction. Translating in diaspora can become an alibi for being absent from the landscape here, and the concerns of its Indigenous people, as settler colonialism has inscribed it in our imaginary as terra nullius.

When we speak of diaspora, we speak of the scattering, but rarely, if ever, of the land that is scattered upon, and so we too reinscribe terra nullius in our relationship to the Canadian landscape. Even refugee settlers appeal to the settler colonial government and international law emerging from settler colonial violence and in so doing legitimize the ideology of manifest destiny that erases the multiple displacements and genocides perpetrated on the Indigenous Peoples of Turtle Island. Confronted with violence all around us, how do we move? How do we act? A path opened up and out through the Indigenous call for "Land Back," which I work with to foreground the relationship to land, the terrain. A sense of accountability to land became a way for me to try to avoid an extractive practice and, instead, make meaningful connections with Indigenous struggles in Turtle Island. I take this methodology into my translation practice where the complex relationships to land that are codified in classical Tamil Sangam literature can be unearthed in contemporary poetry around the war in Lanka. In my own translations, I see how many of the source texts I've worked with serve as archives of relationships to land and landscape that is under erasure even after the war. During our workshops, we lingered on those moments where the literary text acts as an archive of a cultural, historical, or artisanal experience. To translate them with a reverence for the archive seemed to be a form of resistance against the monolithic identities we are compelled to occupy in diaspora. But is that all it can be? Can reverence for the archive become an infinitely inward gaze?

Translation as resistance asks us to look outward, to dwell with an audience in our imaginations as we do the work. Every work of translation is an interpretation of its source text, and the interpretation is not a neutral one. When, during our workshops, I shared that I used Tamil tree names in my translations, one of our participants was surprised. "Why not use the English names?" she asked. When I told her that in some instances there was no English name, she insisted that the correct procedure was to use the Latin species name. "There's a universal term for each tree," she insisted, heatedly. It would be a universal term that was no more familiar to the reader than the Tamil name, I told her. So, what was the point? "The reader can look it up, if they wanted to," she said. "They can just as easily look up the Tamil name," I replied. I couldn't understand why it made her so angry, that this Tamil word could exist in an English text. "It's not translation, then! Because you're still using a foreign word!

You'll lose your audience." But isn't the Latin word foreign too? Was its foreignness neutralized if it was Eurocentric? Was my audience meant to be European? Do we normalize the audiences we translate for to be European, to be white? I don't mean to suggest this person was pursuing whiteness. Rather, I think she saw a kind of rationality in resorting to a so-called "universal" system of classification. While it makes sense in the world of science to follow a procedure, here, we were speaking of art. It hadn't escaped me that this South Asian woman had gone from using the word "name" to the word "term" to describe her preferred nomenclature. There's a subject to object shift that happened there, and I realized she had turned away from me and the chaotic world I somehow came to represent.

Something beautiful happened when we turned toward each other in our workshops and translated for each other as our audience. We made choices that liberated us. We gifted each other the language of our parents, our grandparents, and their ancestors. We made choices to centre relationships to land that could speak across memories of homelands. We found the threads that ran from Bharathiyaar to Tharmini to Kasro—threads of resistance thrumming with meanings that resonated for us. These meanings became interwoven with other struggles around us: histories of slavery spoke to histories of indenture; residential schools spoke to refugees separated from their families. By turning toward each other we found the strength and safety to help decolonize our practices, to understand that we speak to an audience wider than we had thought possible. Resistance here does not mean shutting out but opening up to each other, to allow each other the chance to dwell in our imaginations.

அச்சமில்லை
பாரதி

அச்சமில்லை அச்சமில்லை அச்சமென்ப தில்லையே
இச்சகத்து ளோரெலாம் எதிர்த்து நின்ற போதினும்,
அச்சமில்லை அச்சமில்லை அச்சமென்பதில்லையே
துச்சமாக எண்ணி நம்மைத் தூறுசெய்த போதினும்
அச்சமில்லை அச்சமில்லை அச்சமென்ப தில்லையே
பிச்சை வாங்கி உண்ணும் வாழ்க்கை
பெற்று விட்ட போதிலும்
அச்சமில்லை அச்சமில்லை அச்சமென்ப தில்லையே
இச்சைகொண்ட பொருளெலாம்
இழந்துவிட்ட போதிலும்
அச்சமில்லை அச்சமில்லை அச்சமென்ப தில்லையே

No Fear

Subramaniya Bharathi
Translation by V. Iswarya

No fear, no fear,
no fear of anything.
Even when the universe is
bent upon opposing one—
No fear, no fear,
no fear of anything.
Even if belittled and berated and
bullied by all—
No fear, no fear,
no fear of anything.
Even if one had to stoop to
beg for alms to live at all—
No fear, no fear,
no fear of anything.
Even when one is bereft of
all that one dearly loved—
No fear, no fear,
no fear of anything!

No Fear

Subramaniya Bharathi
Translation by Thamilini Jothilingam

No fear
No fear, fear
no more
The entire world stands
opposed and still

No fear
No fear, fear
no more
The soul made worthless,
slandered and still

No fear
No fear, fear
no more
life turns to begging
and eating, still

No fear
No fear, fear
no more
All that loved
is lost, still

No fear
No fear, fear
no more
NO FEAR

No Fear

Subramaniya Bharathi
Transcreation & Reflection by Regini David

No fear, no fear
Even when you have destroyed our wombs

No fear, no fear
When women's rights are taken away, we raise our hands

No fear, no fear
Sisters unite and become Fire and Water

No fear, no fear
We break through barriers and oppression.

∼

I wrote this as a feminist poem, as women have always been targeted disproportionately in war and all areas of society. I wanted to connect this poem with my experiences as a teenage feminist activist who personally experienced war, and to express what I saw other women facing during this time. I wanted to convey the anger I felt.

As women, we bring life into this world through our wombs, only to watch our creations, in turn, destroy life.

பறக்கடவுள்
சுகிர்தராணி

சொல்லுகிறீர்கள்
முதுகு விரியக் காய்ந்தால்
அதன்பெயர் பறவெயில்
உலரும் புழுத்த தானியத்தை
அலகு கொத்தி விரையும்
அது பறக்காகம்
கையிலிருப்பதை
மணிக்கட்டோடு
பறித்துச் சென்றால்
அது பறநாய்
நிலத்தை உழுது
வியர்வை விதைத்தால்
அது பறப்பாடு
சகலத்திற்கும் இப்படியே
பெயர் என்றால்
இரத்த வெறியில் திளைக்கும்
எது அந்த பறக்கடவுள்.

Pariah God
Sukirtharani
Translation by V. Iswarya

The scorching summer heat
that spreads across your back?
You call it—pariah sun.
What pecks and scats with the
Worm-ridden grain that dries?
You call it—pariah crow.
Grabbing at what you hold,
The beast that rips off your wrist?
You call it—pariah dog.
Tilling the stony soil
And sowing the land with sweat?
You call it—pariah toil.
If every bloody thing had to
bear such a name,
What might one call
The one that wallows in bloodlust—pariah god?

Pariah God
Sukirtharani
Translation by Kalaivani Karunakaran

You say
if the heat is backbreaking
it is a *pariah* sun.

If a crow flies away
pecking the worm-infested grains
it is a *pariah* crow.

If a dog snatches away
what is in the hand along with wrists
it is a *pariah* dog.

If one ploughs the land
sowing one's sweat
it is *pariah* labour.

If everything is named in this way
which is the blood-thirsty *pariah* god?

Pariah God

Sukirtharani
Translation by Subhanya Sivajothy

You tell me that the name of the
heat splintering your back is
the pariah-sun.

It pecks and flees with
dried, worm-infested grain—
a pariah-crow

If it steals away with everything on
your hands, your wrists, then it is
a pariah-dog

To plough the land,
and sow your sweat
that is pariah-pain.

If everything continues
by this name—whose
pariah-god is it
delighting
in this bloody rage?

அமீரின் காதலன்
கஸ்ரோ பொன்னுதுரை

அமீர்,
உனைக் கண்டு
இன்றோடு
ஒருவாரம் ஆகின்றது.

கோடிப்புற
அலரிமரக் கிளையிலிருந்து
காகம் ஒன்று
மூன்று நாட்களாக
கரைந்துகொண்டிருக்கிறது.

அதே மரத்தின் கீழ்தான்
பக்கத்துவீட்டு பாத்திமாவின்
வெள்ளடியன் சேவல்
போன ஞாயிறு அன்று
அஸ்ஸலாத் தொழுகை முடித்து
வீடுதிரும்பிய போது
கண்கள் சிவக்க
மரித்துக்கிடந்தது.

'துர்சகுனம்'
அனா கூறிக்கொண்டாள்

சலீம்
படகேறிச் சென்ற போது
அனா பார்த்த பார்வை.

தன்
கைகளில் படிந்த
முதல் மாதவிடாய் ரத்தத்தினை
முல்லா பார்த்த பார்வை.

அமீர்,
முதல் தருணம்
காதலை உணர்பவனிடமிருந்து
வேறு எதனை எதிர்பார்க்கின்றாய்,
உன்னை
வெறித்துப் பார்த்துக்கொண்டிருப்பதனை விட?
*
கரீபியன் பகுதியிலிருந்து
கீழ்தேசம் வரும்
செந்நிறக் கால்கள் கொண்ட
பிளமிங்கோ பறவைகளை
கபரிஸ்தான் கடற்கரைகளில்
நான்
ஒருபோதும் கண்டதில்லை.

சலீமின் மூத்தமகன் அப்துல்லா
ரசூலின் படகுமேல் நின்ற
இரு பிளமிங்கோ பறவைகளை நோக்கி
வியப்புடன்
'சூரியப் பறவைகள்'
என்ற போது
என் மனம் முழுவதும்
நீயே வியாபித்திருந்தாய்.

அமீர்,
உனது அறையின்
ஜன்னல் வழியே
மும்பை புறநகர் பகுதி
புறாக்களைக் காணும்
நமது கனவை
எண்ணிக்கொண்டேன்.

ஆம்,
இக்கடல்
இவ்வானம்
இப்பறவைகள்
யாவும் நமக்கானதல்ல...

Amir's Lover (excerpts)

Kasro Ponnuthurai
Translation by Yalini Jothilingam

Ana's look
the moment Saleem
boarded the raft

Mulla's look
at the first menstrual blood
coating one's hand

Amir,
what else do you expect
from one who feels love
for the first time,
than
to stare at you.

    *

On Kabristan shores
I have never seen
red-legged flamingos
migrating from the Caribbean to the East

As Saleem's eldest son Abdullah
with awe
called the pair of flamingos on Rasool's raft
"Sun Birds"
it was you who
engulfed my heart.

Amir,
I thought of our dream
to watch the doves
of Mumbai's suburbs
through the windows of your room.

Yes
this sea
this sky
these birds
none are ours.

Amir's Lover (excerpts)

Kasro Ponnuthurai
Translation & Reflection by Subhanya Sivajothy

Amir,
it will be
one week today
since I last saw you.

In the backyard,
on the branches of
an arali tree, a crow
has been croaking
for three days.

When the next-door neighbour Fatima
returned home last Sunday
after finishing her salat,
her fighting cock
with its reddened eyes
lay there dead
underneath that same tree.

They're ill omens
Ana had said.

∾

When I first read "Amir's Lover," I was reminded of the root meaning of the word queer, which evolved from "across." This particular excerpt is part of a longer poem that travels across different terrains—from neighbours' houses to estuaries and beaches—creating landscapes of relation rooted in this address to Amir.

The poem has the quality of an ode; there is a ripeness of bodies and symbolism in its address. Subtext abounds in this poetry, with queer melancholy surfacing through the setting.

There is a natural rhythm to this poem. Like ocean waves, the short lines and stanzas expand into heavier and more imagistic stanzas. The name Amir, repeated as a single line throughout the poem, becomes the sonic backbone that undergirds these landscapes. Even the speaker is referred to in relation to Amir in the title of the poem.

In translation, I've found that the choice of proper names for flora can be a tricky decision. I decided to transliterate the Tamil name for the plumeria or frangipani instead of the name of Latin origin because I thought the sound of it blended well with the names of the people. Arali flowers, symbolic of love and devotion, are often used for worship and are analogous to an ode itself.

Here, the tension between image, mood, and language evocatively reflects the weight of desire, leaving us without any easy answers.

சிறகு விண்ணப்பம்
அக்கினி சுகு

ஒரேயொரு கவிதை
உரக்கப் பாட வேண்டும்
ஊர் வாய்க்காலில் ஓடி
தேச நதிக்குள் விழுந்து
உலகக் கடலில் சங்கமமாக
ஒரேயொரு கவிதை
உரக்கப் பாட வேண்டும்

நால்வர் தோள் கொடுக்க
வாய்க்கரிசி வாங்கிச் செல்லும்
கற்பனை சடலங்கள்
குதித்தெழுந்து நிற்க
ஒரேயொரு கவிதை
உரக்கப்பாட வேண்டும்

முதுகெலும்பு முறிந்த
பின்னும்
விசுவாச தடி ஊன்றி
உடல் சுமக்கும் கூட்டம்
ஒரு பிடி நிமிர
ஒரேயொரு கவிதை
உரக்கப் பாட வேண்டும்

நீராவி நடுவே புட்டு
அவிக்கின்ற
தீராத கனவுகள்
ஒரு நாள்
தொடராமல் போனதும்
அடுத்த கண்டுபிடிப்புக்கு
ஆதாரமாக
ஒரேயொரு கவிதை
உரக்கப் பாட வேண்டும்

A Wing's Request
Akkini Sugu
Translation by Enbah Nilah

I want a single poem
to sing aloud.
Until it runs down the village's canal,
falls into the nation's river,
and merges into the ocean of the world,
I want a single poem
to sing aloud.

Until the corpse of imagination,
shouldered by four people
collecting rice for its mouth,
leaps and stands up,
I want a single poem
to sing aloud.

Until the crowd who lug their bodies,
with faith held up by a crutch
even after their spines were broken,
could lift themselves up a little,
I want a single poem
to sing aloud.

When the dream of puttu cooked in steam
doesn't return one day
as proof of a new discovery,
I want a single poem
to sing aloud.

பாலை உறைய வைத்து
தயிராக்கி கலக்கி
மோராக்கும்
நனவுலக சாசனங்கள்
ஈர்த்து விட்டால்
பின் விடுதலைக்கு வித்திட
ஒரேயொரு கவிதை
உரக்கப் பாட வேண்டும்
அது ஊர் வாய்க்காலில் ஓடி
தேச நதிக்குள் விழுந்து
உலகக் கடலில்
சங்கமமாக வேண்டும்!

If the laws of the material world,
where milk set to curd
and watered down to mor
appeals to us,
then, to sell for freedom,
I want a single poem
to sing aloud
until it runs down the village's canal,
falls into the nation's river,
and merges into the ocean of the world.

---

* mor is buttermilk

230 - Mannar

Abi Jeyaratnam

Mannar maNNil muLaikkum malarkaLin vaasanai enkae?*
thaeni suRum sathathai kaaNoam....
kaaRukkuL oLinthirukkum uNmaikaL ethu?
kathaRalkaalam kaNNirkalam vithaitthha kodumai.
Mannar maNNil muLaitha malarkaLin vaasanai enkae?
Puthaiththa uyirkalin eNNikkai ethanai?
Oayaatha mananGaL, kaayaatha kaayanGaL...
IvarkaLae emathu mannar maNNin malarkaL.
thunpatta nilaiyil inRu em makkaL
uNmaiyum, neetheeyum inaiyum oLiyil,
thirumpi sellum thaeni kuuttam...mannar malarkaLin vaasanai thaedi.

---

* Abi's poems, often recited at public and activist events, are being published and translated here for the first time. We have chosen a conventional transliteration system to avoid linguistic misinterpretation.

230 - Mannar

Abi Jeyaratnam
Translation by Nedra Rodrigo

Where is the fragrance of the flowers that bloom in the soil of Mannar?
We never hear the circling of bees...
What are the secrets hidden in the wind?
Torment sown by the times of wailing and tears.
Where is the fragrance of the flowers that bloom in the soil of Mannar?
How many lives have been buried?
Uneasy hearts, unhealed wounds...
They are the flowers of our Mannar's soil
Our people in the sorrowful moonlight
In the light that unites truth and justice
A swarm of bees turns away...in search of the fragrance of Mannar's flowers.

---

* mor is buttermilk

nhilavil irukkum en appaa
Abi Jeyaratnam

---

nhilavil thanGum en aasai appaa
un aasai makaLin anpu kaditham.
vaaNin neelam un anpin veLichaththil maRaiyum
nhiththam un nhinaivu vanhthu poaka,
maadiyil irunhthu naan anaanthu paarpen
enna kannamma en ullaththin seviyil pathikka.
nii irukkum idam thuuram...
naan aayiram adikal eduththaalum, kittaa thuuram.
aanalum, nee puumiyil vithaiththa nhinaivukaL
en veetu thoattaththil malarnthu paRavum athan vadivu...
intha maadiyin inimai...
ellaam un kaNNamma rasikka.

For Appa Who Lingers in Moonlight
Abi Jeyaratnam
Translation by Nedra Rodrigo

To my beloved Appa who lingers in moonlight,
a letter from your loving daughter.
The blue of the sky would disappear
in the light of your love.
as thoughts of you come and go everyday
I peer down from the balcony, looking for you
My heart hears the sound of "my Kannamma."
You are so far away...
I could not reach you even in a thousand steps.
But the memories you planted on earth
they bloom and spread their beauty in my garden at home...
the sweetness of this balcony...
all for your Kannamma's delight.

நாரைவிடு தூது
சத்திமுத்தப் புலவர்

நாராய்! நாராய்! செங்கால் நாராய்
பழம்படு பனையின் கிழங்கு பிளந்தன்ன
பவளக் கூர்வாய் செங்கால் நாராய்!
நீயுநின் மனைவியும் தென்றிசை குமரியாடி
வடதிசைக் கேகுவீ ராயின்
எம்மூர்ச் சத்திமுத்த வாவியுள் தங்கி
நனைசுவர்க் கூரைக் கணைகுரற் பல்லி
பாடு பார்த்திருக்குமென் மனைவியைக் கண்டு
எங்கோன் மாறன் வழுதிக் கூடலில்
ஆடை யின்றி வாடையின் மெலிந்து
கையது கொண்டு மெய்யது பொத்திக்
காலது கொண்டு மேலது தழீஇப்
பேழையுள் இருக்கும் பாம்பென உயிர்க்கும்
ஏழை யாளனைக் கண்டனம் எனுமே.

Message through the Stork
The Poet of Sathimutham
Translation & Reflection by V. Iswarya

O Stork! O Stork!
O red-legged stork
with pointed coral-red bill
like the split-open sprout
of an aged Palmyra root!
O red-legged stork!
You and your mate,
after you bathe in the southern seas at Kumari,
Should you head northward, tarry awhile
at my native Sathimutham pond;
seek out my worried wife staring for a sign
from the hoarse-hissing house gecko
under the roof over damp walls.
Tell her:
In my King Maaran Vazhudhi's Koodal city
you have seen the poor wretch
naked and weakened by the northerly winds,
his whole body huddled in his hands,
legs drawn up and wrapped in a fold,
surviving like a snake in a casket.

The Home You Carry Within

As I write, Spring arrives in the garden city of Bengaluru and pink trumpet flowers, copper pods, and jacarandas mark the change of season in a riot of colour. Back home in Chennai, Spring was a far more muted affair—it came in unnoticed and disappeared quickly before the scorching summer announced its presence like a loud and annoying house guest who always overstays their welcome. An indefinite period of humid-hot weather, the unbearably hot spell from March to July, and windy wet months with the occasional cyclone were the only seasons I had known growing up; winter was just theoretical. When asked about the pleasant weather and the better career options in my new city, I mumble a few vaguely grateful platitudes to steer the conversation away from what I sorely miss: the certainty of where I belong and the comforting familiarity of foods, smells, sights, and sounds—of people and places that seem to possess an air of permanence.

Perhaps a large part of that permanence comes from its language, which has evolved and shifted shape over thousands of years and yet remained intimate and recognizable as a link in a living tradition. I was unselfconsciously Tamil at home—the fact needed neither proof nor defence. At that time, I barely felt the need to translate except as an occasional academic exercise. After all, everyone in my world was equally Tamil—who would I be speaking to or speaking for? "Bragging to your brother about your birth home," as the saying goes.

The distance between home and a new land becomes palpable in the distance between thought and word. Communication is now a conscious act—of finding equivalences and approximating the word to the feeling. Translating everyday phrases—the price of a coconut, the time the last bus would arrive, the day the cooking gas cylinder would be delivered, a half-gesticulated explanation of what dried manithakkali is to a clueless grocer—made me aware of how language mediates living. Choosing to translate from Tamil, then, became a way of homecoming—to reach for what I had left behind and to carry it consciously with me into another space; shepherding an experience from its cosy, native Tamil expression as safely and sensitively as I could into alien surroundings that could only uneasily accommodate it turned out to be both challenging and comforting.

When I reach back into Tamil history once again through its poetry, I slowly realize that migrating for a living and missing home have always been part of the Tamil experience—be it for the poet from Sathimutham (whose hometown we know, but not his name) or Rashmy, for whom all rain isn't the same.

நாய்களின் அரசியல்
ஆதவன் தீட்சண்யா

நாய்களைப்பற்றி நாமெல்லோரும்
ஒரேமாதிரி நினைப்பதில்லை
நாய்களனைத்தும் ஒரேமாதிரியாய்
இல்லாததைப்போலவே

குரல்வளையைக் கவ்வும் நாய்
குண்டிச்சதையை குதறும் நாய்
சீமாட்டிகள் மடியில் தவழும் நாய்
மாட்டெலும்பு கடித்ததை மறைக்கும் சுத்த சைவநாய்
அபாய அறிவிப்பிலிருக்கும் எலும்பு படத்துக்கே
ஜொள்ளொழுக்கும் ஒரிஜினல் முனியாண்டிவிலாஸ் நாய்
பேட்டைநாய் கோட்டைநாய் வேட்டைநாயென்று
வகையெத்தனையானாலும்
நன்றியில் ஆட்டுவதாய் நம்பப்படும் வால்
பின்பகுதியிலிருக்க
கோபத்தில் கடித்துக் குதறும் வாயோ
எடுத்தயெடுப்பில் முன்பகுதியிலேயே இருக்கிறது.
வாலாட்ட வேண்டுமானால்
குறைந்தபட்சம் தங்கபிஸ்கட்டாவது கொடுத்தாகவேண்டும்
கடிப்பதற்கோ
அவை நாய்களாக இருப்பதாலேயே
காரணங்கள் தேவையற்றதாகிறது.

அரசாங்கம் தண்டிக்கும்போது
நீதிமன்றம் காப்பாற்றும் என்று நம்புவதைப்போன்றே
ஒருநாய்
வெறியில் கடிக்கும்போது
அதன் வால்மட்டும் சுயேச்சையாய் ஆடுமென்று நினைப்பதும்
முட்டாள்தனமாகும்
ஏனென்றால்
வேறுவேறு இடத்திலிருந்தாலும்
வாலும் வாயும் ஒரேநாயின் ஒருங்கிணைந்த உறுப்புகள்.

Politics of the Dogs

Aadhavan Dheetchanya
Translation by V. Iswarya

Of dogs, we all don't think alike
just as dogs themselves aren't alike—
The dog that grabs at the throat
the dog that rips the flesh off the buttocks
the dog that lounges on ladies' laps
the pure vegetarian dog that conceals the taste of cattle bone
the original muniyandivilas dog that drools over
even the image of crossbones in a "Danger" sign
street dog, police dog, hunter's dog...

Although dogs are of several kinds,
their tail believed to be wagged in gratitude
is at the back, while
the mouth that mauls and minces
is right in front.

For the favour of a tail-wag
at least biscuits need be offered,
whereas
their bite requires no particular pretext
since they are dogs anyway.

Just as it is vain to hope
the court would protect one from a government that persecutes,
it is sheer folly to believe that
when a dog bites one in a rabid fit,
the tail alone would wag on its own:
for though they may be at different ends
the mouth and the tail
are integral parts of the same dog.

நிழல் முறிந்த மரம்
எஸ். போஸ்

நாங்கள் கடைசியாக எது பற்றிப் பேசினோம்
மதுவில் மிதந்து கொண்டிருக்கும்
பனிக்கட்டி பற்றியா
வாழ்வு சிதறிய துகள்களிலிருந்த
கண்களைப் பற்றியா?

எனக்கு ஞாபகமிருக்கிறது
அருள் முடிந்து ஓய்ந்து விட்டான் சாமியாடி.
திட்டுத் திட்டாய் குங்குமம் சிதறிக் கிடக்கிறது
வாசல் முழுக்க.
வெற்றிலை வதங்கிப் போயிற்று நரம்புகள் சுருங்கி.
கரிய புகையில் எதையோ யாசித்தபடி
நிற்கிறார்கள் சாமியாடியின் சொற்களில்
கிறங்கிய எல்லோரும்.

எனக்கு ஞாபகமிருக்கிறது
தொட்டுப் பார்க்கும் தூரம் கூட இல்லை இருவருக்கும்.
எனினும்
ஒரு தெருவில் அவர்களும்
இன்னொன்றில் இவர்களுமாய்
நீள்கின்றது எமக்கான தூரம்.

நாங்கள் கடைசியாக எது பற்றிப் பேசினோம்?
நீ எப்போதுமே வெளியே வராத இரவைப் பற்றியா
இருள்
துயர்மிகு இருள்.

Tree with Broken Shade
S. Bose
Translation by Yalini Jothilingam

What did we last talk about
Was it about the ice cube
floating in liquor
or, glistening eyes
in the shattered fragments of life?

I remember
the Saamiyadi resting after his trance
swatches of vermillion scattered
all over the entrance.
Withered betel leaf, with shrunken veins.
Everyone standing in the dark smoke
yearning for something
enchanted by the words of the Saamiyadi.

I remember
we were no further than an arm's reach.
Even so
between us the distance widened
like these ones on one street
and those ones on another.

What did we last talk about?
Was it about the night when you never stepped out
of the dark
the grief-stricken dark.

அன்பு எவ்வாறிருக்கும்
எஸ். போஸ்

நீண்ட நாட்களாய் அது பற்றிய கேள்விகள்
மனதை உலுக்கிச் சிதைக்கின்றன.

சில வேளை வர்ணங்கள் பூசப்பட்ட இனிப்பு மாதிரி,
அல்லது நான் உண்ணும்
உப்பிடாத ரொட்டி மாதிரி
புரியவில்லை.

அதனால் சிந்திக்கவும் கண்ணீர் சிந்தவும்
கொல்லவும் கூட முடியுமாம்,
அயலவர்கள் இவ்வாறு பேசிக் கொள்கிறார்கள்.

எனக்கு அன்பு பற்றி
பாசம் பற்றி
காதல் பற்றி
அயலவரோடு பேச
பயமாயிருக்கிறது.

What Love Looks Like
S. Bose
Translation & Reflection by Yalini Jothilingam

For a long while
questions
shake and shatter the mind.

Sometimes like coloured candies,
or like the saltless roti I eat,
it is unfathomable.

It can think, shed tears
and even kill,
So the neighbours say.

I dread
talking to neighbours
about love
affection
romance.

Shades of Love and Violence
On Translating S. Bose

What is a tree whose shadow has shattered into millions of shards? What becomes of a tree that has lost its ability to cast shade or offer shelter from the blazing sun? What does love—the kind that can think, shed tears, or kill—look like? Or hold? As I read, re-read, sit with, and reflect on the words and images that unfold, I allow myself to be subsumed by S. Bose's haunting poetic scape. The haunting is in the realization that these are not merely abstract, existential, or philosophical questions. Emerging from postcolonial political geographies divided along the ethnic, religious, caste, and many other lines, where everyday violence blurs the boundaries between "us" and "them," these are also deeply political questions that have real impact on human bodies and lives.

S. Bose was murdered in 2007, at the age of 32, in his home in Vavuniya, Sri Lanka, in front of his seven-year-old child. A politically motivated assassination. A life lost too soon, like many. The grief lingers. In words, silences, and voids that are left behind. Like a haunted shadow.

The winding Grand River valley and the rolling hills of Dufferin County, Ontario, which I now call home, unfurl on my way to and back from work. The soft warm rays of the morning sun illuminate the landscape in the mornings, and on my way back, the landscape is often flooded with dusky dark orange shadows. The hills are the traditional territory and ancestral lands of the Tionontati (Pétun), Attawandaron, Haudenosaunee (Six Nations), and Anishinaabe Peoples. The fertile lands nourished by the Grand River are part of the 1818 Ajetance Treaty and Nottawasaga Purchase. The many Indigenous Nations, who once called these lands home, were forced out of their lands by settlers—the rivers and the hills hold on to the silent knowledge and bear witness to the violence, the lingering grief. The poignant vignettes that S. Bose evokes—of trees with broken shades and love that kills—reverberate upon these landscapes as well.

Reading and translating S. Bose has been a humbling process—an act of building critical intimacy with the text and the author, and an awakening to the limits of one's knowledge and interaction with the languages involved. Also, an unrelenting refusal to forget or move on from the wounds inflicted by a violent past.

Language carries the violence. Where ongoing colonial violence has wiped out languages and cultures, the landscape carries the burden of grief. We sit with the language, with the rivers, valleys, and hills to listen, bear witness, and translate. To translate is to remember, to pass on the stories of lives lived, lives lost.

வீடு திரும்புதல்
பா. அகிலன்

தனிமையின் நண்பகலில் பசித்துள்ளேன்

பாறைகளும் பெருங்காற்றும் உதிரத்துள் நகர்கின்றன
உடல் தீ மூண்டு எரிகிறது

மூன்று தசாப்தங்களும் பத்து வருடங்களும்
வைக்க இடமில்லை
வாங்க ஆளுமில்லை
நடக்கிறேன்
காடுகளின் நெடுங்கடலில்
கடந்தகாலம் எங்கோ புதைந்துவிட்டது

இரத்தப் பகல்களை
சிதறித் தெறிந்து பொடிந்து மறையும் உடல்களை
நள்ளிரவுகளிற் பெய்யும் அகாலங்களை
ரணங்கள் மேல் ரணங்கள் தரித்து
காயம் மேல் காயமேற்று புசித்துள்ளோம்

நினைவு ஒரு பாதாளக் குகை

என்ன நிகழ்ந்தது?
வீழ்ச்சியின் விதைகள் எங்கிருந்து வீழ்ந்தன?
ஒரு தசாப்தம் சிறை கிடந்தேன்
திரும்பியபோது தனியனாய் இருந்தேன்
காடாடி
தொடர் இராவுகளை அறுத்து
மீட்ட கிராமம் அந்நியமாய் தோன்றிற்று

இப்போது பசித்துள்ளேன்
உண்ணா நாட்கள் எனை உண்கின்றன
பகலிரவாய்

Homecoming
P. Ahilan
Translation by Kalaivani Karunakaran

My body burns.
Rocks move
in my tempestuous blood.
I am hungry,
on a lonely afternoon.

No place to keep,
and no one to buy,
the three decades and ten years.

I trudge on.
Past was buried
in the depths of the jungles' seas.

We fed
on the blood-red days,
on the bodies
which shattered, scattered,
fragmented, and vanished,
on the doom
pouring through the midnights,
with wounds worn on wounds, and
on scars upon scars.

Memory is an abyss.

What happened?
From where did the seeds of defeat fall?

உன் இறுதிநாளிற் போடாத
பிடி அரிசி
மலையாய் குவிந்து
நத்தை போல பின்னால் ஊருகிறது அம்மா

ஒற்றைக் கண்ணால் அழுகிறேன்

பசி நெடுத்த வயிறு ஓலமிடுகிறது
யாரிடமும் கையேந்தாதே என்றாயே அப்பா

ஊனக்கால் இழுத்து எங்குதான் செல்வேன்

Imprisoned for a decade,
I was alone when I returned.

The village I regained,
traversing the jungles,
cutting across continuous nights,
seems alien now.

I am hungry.
The days I didn't eat
feed on me,
day and night.

Amma, the handful of rice I failed
to offer you on your last day
piles into a mountain, and
trails behind me like a snail.

My single eye weeps.
Hunger-worn stomach howls.

Didn't you say, Appa,
"Don't you ever beg."

But where will I go,
dragging my crippled leg?

purananuru (45)
Subhanya Sivajothy

---

your injury is not from the
eastern white pine
or the tall palmyra,
or garlands of black-branched neem trees
that form atolls around our necks

laburnum rain encloses us both
in its unreadability   until it does not

    you name this demarcation of lineage
    as knowledge. I see a line traced
    to the cliff's edge

when one of us loses, we all lose
when you win, we all lose

and I have seen how the alien waits,
how his cracks are painted like cupfuls

kundalakesi

Subhanya Sivajothy

---

the sentence *what's to wither will wither;*
what's to bloom will bloom flowed onto my desk
amongst notes, glasses, sparrow songs of quiet diction

I unfasten the bloom
let it breathe the filtered air of my apartment, let it weld to my tongue
my paused throat waiting to be unburdened

I want to hear this line as a forgiveness,
it is a fulcrum that coruscates   twitches flutters
like meiosis—half-winged but resolute

its blooms pulsing on the lips with its presence—contesting
my eyes to proceed or abandon

but I'm uncertain how to carry its slippage
how to rest its cuts and bruises on the page

bending my pen, the gelatinous sun shepherds in cargo trucks
what words will I use to flood in all the plovers I'll never see,
who continue to kiss then cast the red loam coasts

the city beyond my window
continues to unfold its blistering symmetry,
as high-pitched peonies gape in their worn balcony pots

it opens me,
the way soft peninsular edges bloom, our dried savannah
dialects bloom
your patchouli perfumed hair and dancing interiors bloom

மழைநாள்
சேரன்

உன் நினைவில் வருகிறதா
அந்த மழைநாள்?

மஞ்சள் வெயிலில்தான் துவங்கி
மழையாகப் போய் முடிந்தது மாலை.
சைக்கிளிலே,
கொஞ்சம் விலகித்தான்
நீ வந்தாய் பக்கத்தில்
எனினும் நிழலிரண்டும் என்னவோ
சேர்ந்தபடிதான் அசைய,
வானம் இருண்டு,
வரம்புகளில்லாத ஒரு மழையில்
நிலத்தில் புழுதி செத்துப் போயிற்று.

தெருவோரச் சிறு குடிலுள்
மழைக்கு ஒதுங்கி முகம் துடைத்தபோது
கைகளும் ஈரம்

உன் நினைவில் வருகிறதா
அந்த மழை நாள்?

நீர் வழிந்து, மை ஊறி
நனைந்துபோன பாடக் குறிப்புகள்
மறுபடியும் எழுதப்படாமலே போயிற்று.

சோர்ந்துபோன மரங்கள்மீதும்
பூவரசமிலைகள் துடிதுடிக்கவும்,
பனை ஓலைகளுடாக வருகிற காற்று
அன்று கடலோடு உறைந்து போகவும்
மழை.

Rainy Day

Cheran
Translation by Jayashree Panicker

Do you remember
that rainy day?

The evening,
having begun in
yellow sunshine,
ended in endless rain.

You rode beside me
on your cycle,
though it wasn't far.
Even as our shadows
mingled, danced,
the sky darkened.
An endless rain
engulfed the dust on the street.

We sought shelter
in a hut nearby.
Our hands dripping
as we wiped our faces.

Do you remember
that rainy day?

Our rain-soaked
ink-streaked lecture notes,
never to be written again.

The wind weaving through
tired trees, trembling portia leaves.

அருகில் நீ.
குடிலுக்குள் நசநசத்த ஈரம்
திரண்டிருந்த விசும்பு மழைக்கறுப்பில்
மின்னல்
கோடாய் எழுந்து அலைந்து அழிகிறது.

கொடிமின்னல் என்று நீ சொல்ல
வான்வெளியை நான் பார்க்கிறேன்.

கணத்துள் அது முடிய
அடுத்ததற்காய்க் காத்திருப்பாய்.
அப்போது இடி முழங்கும்.

மழைச்சாரல் தெறித்த முகத்தில்
நனைந்தபடி நீண்ட மயிரொன்று
கழுத்துவரை, ஒரு
வழி தப்பிய ஆடு.

மழை குறையத் தூற்றல் மனங்கொள்ள
மீண்டும் பயணம்
தெருவோரம்,
மனுஷப் பிசாசுகளின்
விழி விதைத்த பார்வை
அம்புகளாய்க் குத்தும்,
ஈட்டிகளாய்த் துருவும்தான்
எனினும்,
இணை கொண்ட போது
தெருவும் சிதறுகிறது.
மீண்டும் சிறு தூற்றல்
மழை முகிலின் இருள் கவிய
நானும் நீயும் சமாந்தரமாய்...

உன் நினைவில் வருகிறதா
அந்த மழைநாள்?

Palmyra fronds frozen at sea,
becoming rain.

You were beside me,
dampness filled the hut.
In the darkness of the rain,
a band of lightning streaked through the sky,
then vanished.

"Lightning," you exclaimed.
I looked at the sky,
It disappeared in a moment.
We waited for the next one,
then the thunder roared.

A long strand of hair fell
on your rain-soaked face
reaching your neck.
A goat gone astray.

When the rain tapered to a drizzle,
we started again
along the streets.
Human devils stared at us,
their gaze pierced us like falling arrows.

Yet
as we mingled,
the street dispersed.

Again, a small drizzle.
You and I walk together
under dark rain clouds...
Do you remember
that rainy day?

நாம் சுமக்கும் நிலம்
the lands we hold

மார்கழி வன்னி 2012
நிலாந்தன்

காப்பற்சாலை.
சாம்பலையும் கண்ணீரையும் மூடிக்
கம்பளம் விரிக்கப்படுகிறது.

தறப்பாள் வீடுகள்
மழையில் மிதக்கின்றன.

காட்டாறு
கைவிடப்பட்ட காவலரண்களை
அறுத்துப் பாய்கிறது.

உத்தரித்த கிராமங்களிற்கோ
உயிர்ச்சுதை உலர்ந்துவிட்டது.

மார்கழி வன்னி 2012
மிதிவெடிக்குப் பதிலாக
சேப்பங்கிழங்கு விளையுமொரு காலத்தின்
கைபேசி அழைப்பிற்காக
காத்திருக்கிறான்
வன்னி அகதி.

Vanni, December 2012

Nillanthan
Translation by Thamilini Jothilingam

The carpet road.
A blanket is spread
covering ashes and tears.

Tarpaulin houses
float in the rain.

The jungle river
slashes through
abandoned guard posts.

Distressed villages
are dried of soulful ambrosia.

The Vanni refugee
waits for a call
from a time
when unsown fields
grow taro roots
instead of landmines.

வன்னிக்காடு வைகாசி 2013
நிலாந்தன்

வண்ணாத்திப் பூச்சிகள்
கதிர்காமத்திற்குப் போகும் வழி.

சிறுமஞ்சட் பூப்பரவிய
வேட்டை பாதை.

மடுக்காட்டில்
வீரை பழுத்திருக்கும்.

முழங்காவிற் காட்டில்
பாலை பழுத்திருக்கும்.

முறிப்புக்காட்டில்
கொண்டல் பூத்திருக்கும்

பறங்கியாற்றில்
வண்ணாத்திப்பூச்சிகள்
சிறகாறும்

வேட்டைக்காரர்கள் இல்லை
வேட்டைப்பாடல்களும் இல்லை

காவலரணில்
சலித்திருக்கும் சிப்பாயின்
கைபேசி அழைப்பிசை மட்டும்
இடைக்கிடை கேட்கும் காடு

Vanni, May 2013

Nillanthan
Translation by Thamilini Jothilingam

The path that butterflies
take to Katirkamam

A hunting trail full
of small yellow flowers.

In the Matu jungle,
virai ripens

Palai mellows
in the Mulankavil jungle,

In the Murippu jungle,
kontal blossoms

Butterflies rest
their wings
in the Parranki river

There are no hunters
There are no hunting songs

At the guard post
the mobile ringtone
of the weary soldier
is the only music
the jungle hears now and then.

Fraser Valley, December 2023

Thamilini Jothilingam

∼

The sun set at 4:17 p.m. today. I walked on the trail along the Vedder River as the moon was rising above the bare birch trees and the snow-capped Cascade mountains. The pale turquoise Vedder River was rushing past with its whitewater rapids. It has been raining all week. Atmospheric river, they said. Rivers in the sky. Today though, the air was pleasant, fresh and crisp with the scent of the river and the dirt road. The deep red branches of the blueberry bushes added another texture to the landscape. It is called "the valley of many streams" in Halq'eméylem, the language of the Stó:lō communities, the people of the river.

For the first time in my life, I live very close to the mountains. When people asked me before where I would ideally like to live, I always said: "Somewhere between the mountains and the ocean." Now, I feel fortunate to live in this fertile Fraser Valley, the unceded and ancestral territory of the Stó:lō. For someone who was born into and grew up amid a civil war, this valley feels like a tranquil paradise. On the way to work, I see snow-capped Mount Baker shining in the soft morning light. The mist shifts with the winds over the deep blue horizon of the surrounding mountains. Farm country is a few blocks from the centre of town, with farms after farms after farms the furthest your eyes can see. This valley is the berry capital of Canada, the breadbasket of British Columbia. In the summer, all the flowers, the berries, the wild grasses are in full bloom and alive. It's quite interesting how the lands in which you live, the lands that you left, the lands on which you walk, like an expansive prairie sky, like a spell, all grow in you, with you.

The story of this valley is also the story of colonial violence, from the Fraser Canyon Gold Rush of 1858 to the construction of the Canadian Pacific Railway in the 1880s. The extractive industries that drove this province's economy transformed these lands drastically and displaced its Indigenous communities. Not far from where I walked earlier today, the land that holds an exhaustive number of farms between the Sumas and Vedder mountains was once a lake—Sumas Lake—an area of roughly 30,000 acres changing rapidly with seasons and full of thriving indigenous flora and fauna, including the highly nutritious blue-joint grass that can grow as tall as four to six feet.

In November 1828, Francis Annance, the first European who stood on the lake, reported back to his superior, Archibald McDonald, the chief trader at Hudson's Bay Company at Fort Langley:

> About 25 miles up they turned into a small creek to the right which in a few hours brought them to a lake of 10 miles long and 6 wide at the extreme end of which there is a considerable extent of low clear Country—intersected with numerous ponds and little Channels well adapted for wild fowl—here they spent the best part of two day[s] and killed 4 Swans 3 Cranes 10 Geese & 40 ducks.[1]

---

[1] Chad Reimer. *Before We Lost the Lake.* Halfmoon Bay: Caitlin Press, 2018. 66

John Lord, a veterinary surgeon who was part of the Northwest Boundary Survey and who arrived in the Sumas Valley in 1859, wrote:

> Our camp was on the Sumass prairie, and was in reality only an open patch of grassy land, through which wind numerous streams from the mountains, emptying themselves into a large shallow lake, the exit of which is into the Fraser by a short stream, the Sumass river. In May and June this prairie is completely covered with water: The Sumass river; from the rapid rise of the Fraser, reverses its course, and flows back into the lake instead of out of it. The lake fills, overflows, and completely floods the lower lands. On the subsistence of the waters, we pitched our tents on the edge of a lovely stream. Wildfowl were in abundance; the streams were alive with fish; the mules and horses reveling in grass kneedeep—we were in a second Eden![2]

In 1924, the lake was drained, which was celebrated as an engineering feat of the time. The land was transformed into farmlands for European settlers and their families. In the fall of 2021, I arrived in the Fraser Valley in the middle of an atmospheric river rain and heavy floods, when the lake reclaimed the farmlands for a few weeks.

*

The dyke trail along the Vedder River was built on the soil excavated from the now extinct lake. Walking on it earlier today somehow reminded me of a walk along the embankment of the Padaviya tank in Vanni a few years ago. The two share long and winding dirt paths along the waters, tall waving grasslands, homes to many birds. It was the last time I was in Sri Lanka before the pandemic. On a sweltering day in June, I had

---

[2] Chad Reimer. *Before We Lost the Lake*. Halfmoon Bay: Caitlin Press, 2018. 66

convinced my thambi to drive to Padaviya. We set out early in his small white delivery lorry from Vavuniya. When we turned into Padaviya Road at the Kebithigollewa junction, my heart started beating faster. We passed a few military checkpoints. I had a camera with multiple lenses and audio equipment in the back. I had been away from the country for a while, and my Sinhalese was rusty—and someone from the largest Tamil diaspora in Toronto wandering around Padaviya was bound to raise suspicion. I didn't want to be stopped, and fortunately, my thambi's unassuming lorry helped. Since independence, Padaviya has become a contested territory. One of the early colonization schemes of the postcolonial Sri Lankan state was implemented on this land. The political borders were redrawn multiple times over the past centuries, and it is now part of the Sinhalese-dominated Anuradhapura District. During the last years of the civil war, it was where the Kebithigollewa massacre happened. Centuries before that, it was the ancestral territory of the Tamils. The original name of the tank was a Tamil name: Pativil Kulam (பதிவில் குளம்).

We were in search of the ruins of an ancient Tamil town, Pathonnaru Nakaram (பதொன்னரு நகரம்), that was once situated near the tank. Ainooruvar (அஞ்ஞூற்றுவர்) referred to it as Ayyampollil Pattinam (அய்யம்பொழில் பட்டினம்).[3] A deed from the twelfth or the thirteenth century refers to it as Sripati village (சிறீபதி கிராமம்). This town was strategically situated in the midpoint of the North Central Province, between the two major harbours to the east and west and was thought to have been built between the sixth and tenth centuries. An early archaeological excavation in the 1950s documents the ruins of the earliest

---

[3] P. Schalk and A. Velupillai. eds. *Buddhism among Tamils in Pre-Colonial Tamilakam and Ilam*, Part 2: The Period of the Imperial Cholar—Tamilakam and Ilam. Uppsala: Uppsala University, 2002. 706.

Sivan temple, Iravikulamanikka Isvaramutaiyar Sivathevalayam (இரவிகுலமாணிக்க ஈஸ்வரமுடையார் சிவதேவாலயம்), older than that of the Polonnaruwa period and significant Tamil epigraphs. Historical and archaeological evidence reveals the presence and influence of Tamil merchant groups in the area, but now there are no records of the existence of this temple or the town or the Tamil epigraphs. The whereabouts of the archaeological findings are still a mystery.

My thambi and I walked along the embankment, back and forth, as the Vanni hot winds rose through our black Bata slippers. There wasn't a single soul around. There were no ruins. No heritage sites. Not even an inscription. I had a piece of a printed satellite map that I had found on a random site online. It was the only evidence I had of the ruins. We circled the country roads again a few times to no avail. On the way back, we drove through the lush farmlands of Padaviya with sophisticated ancient irrigation systems and canals. On every corner, often under tall trees, were small Pillaiyar statues. Under the statues, in Sinhalese, the inscriptions read, "Gana deiyo."

In 1848, James Emerson Tennent, the resident Colonial Secretary of Ceylon, travelled to the banks of Padaviya. He writes:

> Before daybreak we entered on the bed of the tank of Padivil, at its south-eastern angle, and proceeded towards the main embankment, a ride which occupied us nearly two hours. The tank itself is the basin of a broad and s[h]allow valley, formed by two lines of low hills that gradually sink into the plain as they approach towards the sea. The extreme breadth of the enclosed space may be twelve or fourteen miles, narrowing to eleven at the spot where the retaining bund has been constructed across the valley; and when this enormous embankment was in effectual repair, and the reservoir filled by the rains, the water must have been thrown back along the basin of the valley for at least fifteen miles.[4]

The land comes to life as he further documents:

> In a lonely spot, towards the very centre of the tank, we came unexpectedly upon an extraordinary scene. A sheet of still water, two or three hundred yards broad, and about half a mile long, was surrounded by a line of tall forest-trees, whose branches stretched above its margin. The sun had not yet risen, when we perceived some white objects in large numbers on the tops of the trees, and as we came nearer we discovered that a vast colony of pelicans had formed their settlement and breeding-place in this solitary retreat... Nor was this all; along with the pelicans prodigious numbers of other water-birds had selected this for their dwelling-place, and covered the trees in thousands, standing on the topmost branches: tall flamingoes, herons, egrets, storks, ibises, and other waders.[5]

*

My life has been constantly transient since we were first forced to flee from Jaffna in the late 1980s, three weeks after my third birthday. Since then, I have lived on three continents and in eighteen rental houses. It is like being on a cloud, always floating and never grounded, and ready to drift to wherever the storm of time would push me/us. Anytime. The two places that have left a deep imprint on me are Vanni and the Fraser Valley: one, an expansive jungle in the dry zone in the North Central Province of Sri Lanka, the other, an expansive fertile valley near the Pacific west coast of British Columbia, Canada. Two lands colonized by an empire, by two companies—the empires that divided the lands, the people. The violence that is imprinted on the ecologies and natural heritage, and the trauma that we carry through and on these lands are the lingering specters of colonialism. The

---

[4,5] J. E. Tennent. *Ceylon: An Account of the Island Physical, Historical, and Topographical, Vol. II.* London: Longman, 1860. 502-503

irony of it all is that we have to refer to colonial accounts for detailed descriptions of what these places were once, before their drastic historical transformations.

Nillanthan's Vanni poems speak to me in an intimate way. I don't have any childhood memories of Jaffna, where I was born. I thought I did until, after almost seventeen years of being away, I returned to Jaffna alone and travelled with my cousins when the A9 road re-opened following the ceasefire agreement in the early 2000s. My cousin took me on his bike to Amma's village where I had spent my early childhood. As we turned from the main road, my cousin stopped the bike and asked with a smile, "Do you remember the roads? Do you want to show me the way and your house?" I remember feeling a sudden heaviness, as I could not remember anything.

I stared at the sandy road in front of us with neatly woven palymra veli and houses with iron gates with peeling red paint. I couldn't remember the first house that I breathed in, the yard where I first walked and ran around, or the soft sand in which I wrote the first alphabet—my first years in this world. The house my Appappa built with a light green facade and veranda. The row of red and pink hibiscus trees along the front, the pomegranate trees on the side of the house, the murungai trees all around with long hanging clustered white flowers, the tall wood apple tree in the back whose roots extended to Chithi's bathroom next door and broke the ground. The jackfruit tree under which I parked my bicycle, the bicycle Appappa built by hand with adult sized bike wheels. The evenings that I sat on Appappa's lap and read the bold titles of the newspapers he brought from town. The pomegranates that were supposed to be offered to the village temple that ended up in my hands, aunties sneaking those just for me. Those memories were not mine. It was a difficult realization. All the years of being displaced, being far away from that land, I seemed to have carried only the memories of my parents, uncles, and aunts, in the photographs, from the news. I did not have a memory of my own of my early childhood.

The earliest and most profound memory that I have of a land, is of Vanni. In the 1990s, my mother's sister, my Chithi, lived on the outskirts of Vavuniya. She was the only relative that we had a close relationship with during that time. I spent many months of school holidays there without my parents, which, in a way, helped the bond that I formed with the land in my own way. My Chithi had two young children, a quite prolific garden, and a chicken coop. Her neighbours had a daughter, just a year older than me. We instantly became friends. The land, the jungle around—we wandered every inch of it. I didn't understand before when Appa boasted about his soil, the sembaddu mann of his village, and how they would be soaked in red after playing outside and the color would not go away, even after several baths. The Vanni soil was the closest that I came to experiencing that soaking. Vanni soil was not red or wet. It was mostly dry, soft, and hot. Your feet would boil if you stepped on the soil barefoot at midday.

Chithi taught me the names of the trees that stood majestically in the jungles, providing shade from the blistering sun. My friend showed me how to pick the best palai and naval fruits. We ran around the small sandy lanes and out of the residential sections, chasing jungle fowl and squirrels. We experimented with the best ways to brine fresh cashew fruits, separating the nuts and secretly making a fire behind an abandoned house to roast the nuts without getting the black sticky stain on our t-shirts. We climbed the guava trees, ate half the fruit and left the rest for the birds and squirrels. We rode the adult bicycles with a tilt and with one leg under the crossbar, as we were not quite tall enough to sit on the seats. I fell and scraped my knees and ankles a few times and still have the scars from those adventures. At the end of the day, our entire bodies would be soaked in puluthi, and we would run straight to the well and pour a few buckets of cold water from the metal buckets. Vanni gave me the childhood that I had previously lost. I lived those moments carefree while Annamar and Akkamar around me were fighting for that land, from the interiors of the same jungles.

As an adult, I returned to Vanni many times. The first time I crossed the interior was in the early 2000s when the A9 reopened after its first closure in 1984, and I tagged along with my cousins to go to Jaffna. We took the evening bus from Colombo with a stopover in Vavuniya. We arrived at the Omanthai checkpoint in the middle of the night. The checkpoint opened at 5:00 or 6:00 a.m. The bus driver parked the bus in the long queue of vehicles. We all got down and waited for daybreak and the checkpoint to open. There weren't any buildings around. The outlines of the A9 road disappeared into the darkness of the Vanni jungle. I remember looking at the dark sky and for the first time seeing so many stars. The chill of the early morning air that I breathed in seemed unusually familiar. Since then, I always returned to Vanni, and traversed the interior from Madu to Mullaitivu as the kaadu grew in me.

A few years ago, post-war, I went to see a friend's Amma in Palai. She is the patron of a small Vairavar temple. I don't usually feel emotional about temples, but this was different. The temple was situated near a small kulam with a scattered grove of tall palmyra trees on the horizon. It was a semi-open style temple with an ancient tree in the middle. The leaves on the trees glistened with the rays of sun. The sand under our feet was so soft to walk on. We went on a day that was special, although I now don't remember what it was, and they gave us kulai saatham. Thambi and I sat on a fallen tree branch and ate the rice, listening to the faint sound of the kovil mani in the wind. It was a very peaceful and serene environment. I was thinking to myself that if all temples were like this, I wouldn't mind going to temples often. My friend hadn't been back there for a while, so I took some pictures to share with them. When I was describing the natural environment, they said it used to be even nicer when they were growing up on that land. We don't really see or talk about the environmental and ecological cost of war.

What drew me to Nillanthan's poems is that essence—the natural heritage and ecologies that he documents through his words—of Vanni, the kaadu, the trees, the hunting trail with yellow flowers. The way Nillanthan's poems witness the power of nature—jungle rivers reclaiming the lands and lakes, flowing past abandoned guard posts—is a testament to history from an alternative vantage point. The sense of place that his poems evoke within the interiors of ourselves is, I find, deeply moving. They say only Zen and Taoist monks used to be that attentive to the natural environment, the minute details of it all—the enveloping magic of experiencing a particular moment. All those moments. The world—the beautiful poetic harmony among all.

acknowledgements

We would like to thank all the lovely people who participated in our workshops, including those who could not stay on until the end due to their other commitments. We have learned so much from all of you, and your contributions have helped us shape this book, as well as our practices.

We would also like to thank the Tamil poets who consented to having their works being brought into this space of play and experimentation. Your generosity of spirit is a gift to the endurance of the Tamil language, and to the children of the diaspora who continue to find a home in its embrace.

Deep gratitude to Indigenous poets shalan joudry and Leanne Betasamosake Simpson, and their publishers, for granting us permission to present their original poems in English here, alongside our Tamil translations. shalan joudry's poems appear in *Generations Re-merging* (Gaspereau Press, 2014.) Leanne Betasamosake Simpson's poems appear in *Islands of Decolonial Love* (ARP Books, 2015). Warm thanks to shalan, in particular, for thoughtful conversations on decolonial practices in translating Indigenous poetry.

Many thanks to the intrepid team at *trace* who worked through the multiple drafts of this book and its cover design.

And above all, thank you Nuzhat, for daring to dream with us as we stepped into new terrains and new modes of thinking around translation; your solidarity has withstood some tough moments, and your vision has brought us through to the other side. We could not have gone on this journey with anyone else.

contributors

Aadhavan Dheetchanya is a Tamil writer of poetry and fiction. He currently serves as the General Secretary of the Tamil Nadu Progressive Writers and Artists Association. His works often present a mordant criticism of contemporary politics, Hindutva ideology, and the caste system. He lives in Hosur, India.

Abi Jeyaratnam is a second-generation daughter of the Eelam diaspora, living in Tkaranto. She is a multidisciplinary artist who loves to hear, hold, and share stories passed on by elders and community, preserving and unravelling these inherited truths toward healing and liberation.

Akkini Sugu (Sugurmar Velladurai) was a Tamil journalist and poet well known in Malaysia for his articles and commentaries on science, technology, sports, and world politics. He was one of the early proponents of "Puthukavithai" or modern Tamil poetry in Malaysia.

Alari (Abdul Latif Mohammad Rifaz) is a Muslim Tamil poet from the east of Lanka. He has published five collections: *Poomikkadiyil vaanam* (*The Sky Beneath the Earth*, 2005), *Paravai pol sirakadikkum kaadhal* (*Love that Flutters Wings Like a Bird*, 2006), *Ella pookkalum uthirnthuvidum* (*All the Flowers Will Fade*, 2008), *Thulliyallathu thukal* (*A Speck or a Particle*, 2021), and *Perukku* (*Multiply*, 2022). Alari's poetry examines notions of power and powerlessness and chronicles the experiences of Tamil Muslims at the hands of the Liberation Tigers of Tamil Eelam (LTTE), among other things.

Ammoovanar is a poet whose work appears in Tamil classical anthologies of the Sangam period (300 BC–300 AD).

Avvaiyar is a poet whose work appears in Tamil classical anthologies of the Sangam period (300 BC–300 AD).

Cheran (Rudhramoorthy Cheran) was born in the village of Alaveddy, near Jaffna in Tamil Eelam. He is one of the best known and most influential of contemporary Tamil poets, and his poems have been translated into several languages. Cheran co-edited a landmark anthology of Tamil political poetry, *Maranatthul vaallvoom* (*We Live Amidst Death*), in 1985. His early poems were collected in *Nii ippoludhu irangum aaru* (*The River into which You Now Descend*, 2000), *Miindum kadalukku* (*Once Again, the Sea*, 2004), and in *Kaadaatru* (*Funeral Rites*, 2011). He is an Associate Professor of Sociology at the University of Windsor, Ontario. His academic publications include *The Sixth Genre: Memory, History and the Tamil Diaspora Imagination*, and *History and the Imagination: Tamil Culture in the Global Context*, co-edited with Dharshan Ambalavanar and Chelva Kanaganayakam.

Enbah Nilah Sugurmar is an educator, poet, and researcher in Malaysia. Her interest lies in the almost(s) and not-quite(s)—the grey, in-between regions of un-belonging. Her creative works can be found in the *Anthology of Southeast Asian Eco-writing* (*Manoa Journal*, University of Hawai'i Press), *This is Southeast Asia* (AUS), *Innovation for Change-East Asia*, and *Adi Magazine*.

Geetha Sukumaran is a Tamil poet and a bilingual translator and scholar. Her award-winning poetry collection *Otrai pakadaiyil enchum nampikkai* was published in 2014. She translated a selection of P. Ahilan's poetry in *Then There Were No Witnesses* (2018), and collaborated with Ahilan and the artist Vaidekhi on the bilingual collection, *Tea: A Concoction of Dissonance* (2021). Her poems, translations, and essays have appeared in *Still We Sing: Voices on Violence Against Women*, *Beltway Poetry Quarterly*, the art installation *Rucksack*, and in *River in an Ocean: Essays on Translation* (trace, 2023). She is the co-founder of the Conflict and Food Studies Group and is currently a Postdoctoral Fellow at the Culinaria Research Centre at the University of Toronto-Scarborough.

Gobiga Nadanarajah was born in Jaffna. Like many Eelam Tamils, she had to flee from her homeland due to the civil war. She has always felt a strong pull toward her motherland and language even though she left Eelam as a baby. Inspired by her parents, she has been working in the field of Refugee Law for more than 15 years and works primarily with Toronto's Tamil diaspora. She rediscovered her love for poetry when she found a book with poems that she had written as a child. She enjoys exploring the use of words as art to create awareness, to preserve history/heritage, or sometimes to send subtle or bold social messages.

Jayashree Panicker is a writer and literary translator based in Singapore. Her writing has been featured in the *Quarterly Literary Review of Singapore*, *The Epigram Books Collection of Best New Singaporean Short Stories: Vol. 5*, and *Mahogany Journal*.

Kalaivani Karunakaran is a freelance translator, editor, and independent scholar. *Jahanara: A Novel* (2024), marks her debut English translation. Kalaivani earned her doctorate from the Department of English, University of Madras, with a focus on Literary Spatial Studies. She is interested in cross-disciplinary research, intersecting Classical Tamil Studies, Science, and Economics. A versatile artist, she plays the veena, performs as a Carnatic vocalist, and is a practitioner of Kalaripayattu, the ancient martial art of Kerala. She is currently developing a creative curriculum aimed at children's education in India.

Kasro Ponnuthurai is a Tamil poet and cultural activist. His literary influences include the poet Ahilan, with whose landscapes he feels a strong connection, and the feminist writings of Perundevi. His poems have appeared in the newspaper Veerakesari, the magazine, *Palmanam*, and online in *Jaffna Sangam*, and in translation in the anthology *Out of Sri Lanka* (2023). His interest in the ways in which Tamil queer art is produced and circulated across South Asia led him to found the Jaffna Queer Festival (JFQ) as a way to build local creativity alongside global connections.

Leanne Betasamosake Simpson is a renowned Michi Saagiig Nishnaabeg musician, poet, writer, and academic, widely recognized as one of the most compelling Indigenous voices of her generation. Her work breaks open the boundaries between story and song, bringing audiences into a rich and layered world of sound, light, and sovereign creativity. She has written eight books, including a *Short History of the Blockade* and the novel *Noopiming: The Cure for White Ladies*, which was short-listed for the Governor General's Literary Award for fiction and the Dublin Literary Prize. Her collaboration with Robyn Maynard, *Rehearsals for Living*, was short listed for the Governor General's Literary Award for nonfiction. She recently published *Theory of Water*.

Nedra Rodrigo is an award-winning translator, scholar, and curator of multi-art events. She is the founder of the Tamil Studies Symposium in Toronto, and the bilingual event series, The Tam Fam Lit Jam. Her translations include *In the Shadow of the Sword* (2020) and the Devakanthan quintet, *Prison of Dreams* (2021–2024) for which she received the 2025 Tamil Literary Garden's Translation award. She has published critical essays in *Briarpatch, C Magazine, Studies in Canadian*

Literature, Human Rights and the Arts: Essays on Global Asia, and in *River in an Ocean: Essays on Translation* (trace, 2023). Her translations of Tamil poetry have appeared in *Words and Worlds, Jaggery Lit, Still We Sing: Voices on Violence Against Women* (2021), and *Out of Sri Lanka* (2023). Her translation of Rashmy's *Songs in a Time of Confinement* received the inaugural PEN Translates x SALT award and will be published by trace in 2026.

Nillanthan is an artist, activist, political analyst, and art critic. He lives and works in Yalpanam, Sri Lanka. His publications include six collections of poetry in Tamil: *Yugapuram* (*The Epic of an Age*), *Kanji paadal* (*The Songs of Kanji*), and *Yugamudivum pinnarum* (*End of an Age and After*). His political essay collections include, *Pulikalukku pinnaraana arasiyal* (*Politics After the Tigers*, 2017) and *Ninaivukalai thalaimuraikaloodu kadathal* (*Transmitting of Memories across Generations*, 2020). Translations of his poems have appeared in various anthologies. His artworks, *Bunker Family Series, Ravana*, and *Pillaiyar: War Portraits*, have been exhibited widely across the subcontinent, and featured in *A to Z of Conflict* (2019).

P. Ahilan (Packiyanathan Ahilan) was born in Jaffna, Sri Lanka. He is a poet, literary and art critic, arts curator, and academic. He received a PhD from Jawaharlal Nehru University of Delhi and teaches art history at the University of Jaffna. His poetry collections include *Pathunkukuzhi naatkal* (*Bunker Days*, 2001), *Saramakavigal* (*Elegies*, 2011), *Ammai* (*Mother*, 2017), and *Azh kadal mazhai* (*Rain in the Deep Sea*, 2024). Geetha Sukumaran translated a selection of his poems into English in *Then There Were no Witnesses* (2018) and collaborated with Ahilan and the artist Vaidekhi on *Tea: A Concoction of Dissonance* (2021). His poetry installation, *One and Many: Forms of Words and Silence*, was exhibited in Jaffna and Colombo in 2021.

Rashmy (Mohamed Rashmy Ahamed) is a journalist, poet, and visual artist. He was born in Akkaraipattu on the East Coast of Lanka, in 1974 and worked with the Tamil newspaper Sarinigar in Jaffna from 1995-2000 before being forced to flee to the UK. His four collections of poetry in Tamil include *Kaavukollappatta vaazhvu* (*Sacrificed Life*), *Aayiram kiraamangalai thindra aadu* (*The Goat that Ate a Thousand Villages*), *Eethenin paambukal* (*Serpents of Eden*) and *E thanathu peyarai maranthu ponathu* (*E Forgot Its Name*). His first collection of short stories, *Satru periya kathaikalin thokuppu* (*A Collection of Slightly Bigger Stories*) received the Tamil Literary Garden's 2024 Award for Fiction. Nedra Rodrigo's translation of *Adaivukaalathin paadalkal* (*Songs in a Time of Confinement*) will be published by trace in 2026.

Regini David began her work in social justice as a teenage activist in Jaffna and Batticoloa during the civil war, where she helped found the women's groups Poorani and Sooriya. Since her arrival as a refugee in Tkaronto, she has worked as a worker's rights advocate, union organizer, and paralegal with a commitment to refugee, labour, legal, and housing rights. She is currently working on a poetry collection as well as a memoir.

S. Bose (Sandrabose Suthagar) is a writer, poet, and journalist from Sri Lanka. He has worked for journals and newspapers such as *Veliccham, Aatharam, Eelanatham, Eelanadu, and Veerakesari*. His works have been published in journals based in Sri Lanka and India. He edited and published the poetry journal *Nilam*, and was the editor of *Thamil ulagam*, a UK-based journal.

Sathimutha Pulavar is a poet who lived in the village of Sathimutam in present-day Tamil Nadu in Southern India. His original name and the period in which he wrote are both unknown.

shalan joudry is a Mi'kmaw poet, playwright, oral storyteller, musician and filmmaker. She has published two books of poetry, *Generations Re-merging* (2014) and *Waking Ground* (2020) and has produced several plays. Joudry starred as all the characters in her play *KOQM* which won Best New Nova Scotian Play at the Robert Merritt Awards. She is a PhD candidate at the Dalhousie University and works as an ecologist, managing programs for species at risk. She has directed and produced a short film, *welima'q*, which premiered at the Toronto Film Festival in 2024.

Subhanya Sivajothy is a librarian and writer living in Tkaronto. She uses poetry to think about ecologies, archives, and struggle. Her work has appeared in *Filling Station* and *Adi Magazine* and has received funding from the Canada Council of the Arts. Her debut poetry collection, *The Certainty of Dust*, will be published by trace in 2027.

Subramaniya Bharati was born in 1882 in Ettayapuram in British India (present day Southern Tamil Nadu). An acclaimed Tamil writer, poet, journalist, social reformer and Indian independence activist, he made significant contributions to the shaping of modern Tamil prose. The Zamin of Ettayapuram gave him the title "Bharati" for his poetic excellence, and he is often referred to as "Mahakavi Bharatiyaar" (the Great Poet). Celebrated for his revolutionary voice, his songs and poems continue to be set to music, recited at protests, and performed in theatres, concerts, and the cinema. Some of his most notable works are *Kannan paattu* (*The Song of Kannan*), *Kuyil paattu* (*The Song of Cuckoo*), and *Panchali sapatham* (*The Vow of Panchali*).

Sukirtharani is a poet widely acclaimed for her contributions to contemporary Dalit and Tamil literature in India. She has published eight collections, including *Iravu mirugam* (*The Night Beast*, 2004), *Theendapadaatha mutham* (*Untouched Kiss*, 2010),

Avalai mozhipeyarththal (*Translating Her*, 2012), and recently, a complete collection of her poetry, *Sukirtharani kavithaikal* (1996–2006). Her works focus on the Dalit movement and feminism and speak against many forms of oppressions and injustices. She has won several accolades including the Tamil Literary Garden Award for Poetry. Her poems have been translated into various languages such as English, Malayalam, Telugu, Oriya, Bengali and German, and a museum for poetry in Florence, Italy, has exhibited one of her handwritten Tamil poems.

Thamilini Jothilingam is an archivist, documentary artist, and translator living and working on the unceded and ancestral territories of the Halq'eméylem-speaking peoples. Her interdisciplinary practice centred at the confluence of art, historiographies, and ethnographic research with a focus on digital memory, social, visual and oral histories, and community-driven heritage work. Thamilini has collaborated with academic and community organizations globally, spearheading documentary and preservation projects.

Tharmini was born in Velanai island off the coast of Jaffna peninsula. She moved to Europe during the civil war and currently lives in France with her family. She began writing poetry in 1992 in local magazines and newspapers in Jaffna. She has published three volumes of poetry in Tamil, *Saavukalaal pirapalamaana oor* (*The Village Famed for Death*, 2010), *Irul mithakum poikai* (*Ponds on which Darkness Floats*, 2016), and *Ayalaal* (*The Neighbour Woman*, 2021). Her next collection is forthcoming in 2025.

V. Iswarya is a freelance critic and literary translator based in Bengaluru. She teaches English literature at the Manipal Academy of Higher Education. She was a South Asia Speaks fellow for translation in the class of 2024 and her translations have twice been shortlisted for the Mozhi Prize. Her critical writings and her translations of B. Jeyamohan's essays have appeared in the national magazine *Frontline*. Her first book-length translation was Perumal Murugan's memoir *Students Etched in Memory* (2025).

Yalini Jothilingam is a poet, writer, and performing artist based in Toronto. Her poetry collection in Tamil *Maranamoorum kanavukal* (*Dreams that Weave Death*, 2016) and Tamil co-translation of *Black Woman's Manifesto* (2017) were published by Anangu Feminist Publication, India. English translation of her poems have appeared in *City: A Quarterly Journal of South Asian Literature* (2017) and *Still We Sing: Voices on Violence Against Women* (2021). She is a doctoral student in the Department of Humanities at York University, Toronto. Her literary and scholarly interests revolve around life writing, religion, political conflicts, and gendered transgressions.

credits

Aadhavan Dheetchanya. "Naaigalin Arasiyal," *Dalit-8*. Vizhupuram: Manarkeni Publications, November 2003.

A. K. Ramanujan. *Poems of Love and War: From the Eight Anthologies and the Ten Long Poems of Classical Tamil*. New Delhi: Oxford India Paperback, 1996.

Ainkurunuru. Chennai: Tamilmann, 2008.

Akkini Sugu. *Iraiya Iru Kanaa*. Selangor: Bathmini Sugumar, 2021. (Self-published)

Alari. *Mazhaiyai Mozhithal*. Nagercoil: Kalachuvadu Pathippagam, 2009.

Cheran. *Nee Ippozhuthu Irangum Aaru*. Nagercoil: Kalachuvadu Pathippagam, 2007.

Kasro Ponnuthurai. "Amiirin Kaathalan." *Paalputhumai*, June 30, 2020. https://www.paalputhumai.com/ameerin-kathalan/

Kurunthokai, edited by K. Ilavazhagan. Chennai: Tamilmann, 2008.

Leanne Betasamosake Simpson. *Islands of Decolonial Love*. Winnipeg: ARP Books, 2015.

M. Pusparajan. *Ampa: Essays on Fishermen's Folk Songs*. Jaffna: Alai Literary Circle, 1976.

Nillanthan. *Yuga Mudivum Pinnarum*. Surrey: Maanudam Foundation, 2023.

P. Ahilan. "Veedu Thirumputhal." (Unpublished)

Sandrabose Suthagar. *S. Bose Padaippukal: Mattrum S. Bose Pattiyum Avarudaiya Padaippukal Pattiyum*. Chennai: Vadaly Veliyeedu, 2016.

Sathimutha Pulavar. "Naaraividu thuuthu." https://www.tamilvu.org/courses/hg300/hg304/html/hg304tso.htm

shalan joudry. *Generations Re-merging*. Nova Scotia: Gaspereau Press, 2014.

Subramanya Bharati. *Bharatiyaar Kavithaigal*, edited by Padmadevan. Chennai: Karpagam Puthagalayam, 2018.

Sukirtharani, *Iravumirugam*. Nagercoil: Kalachhuvadu Pathippagam, 2010

Thandayutham. R, *Malasiya Naatuppura Paadalgal*. Chennai: Tamil Puthakalayam, 1998

Tharmini. *Ayalaal*. Chennai: Karuppu Piradhigal, 2020.

t r a c e is both verb and noun; act and residue.

t r a c e collaborates with writers to publish books that illuminate, in complex, beautiful, and thought-provoking ways, contemporary and historical experiences of conflict, war, displacement, exile, migration, the environment, labour, and resistance.

We look for words that draw connections between here and there; now and then. Voices that ask us to question, reflect, take pleasure, love, remember, and build solidarity across our many differences.

We are unafraid to mix genres, voices, and languages.

t r a c e is a not-for-profit press.

We invite you to support our work.

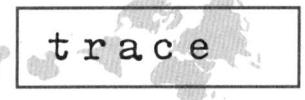

tracepress.org